D0061481

Jeff Kassebaum

ABOUT THE AUTHOR

MICHAEL E. GERBER is the legend behind the E-Myth series of books, which includes *The E-Myth Revisited, E-Myth Mystery, Awakening the Entrepreneur Within, The E-Myth Manager, The E-Myth Physician,* and *The E-Myth Contractor.* His titles have collectively sold millions of copies worldwide. He is an entrepreneur and an in-demand speaker and consultant. Gerber is also the founder of E-Myth Worldwide, Chief Dreamer Enterprises, In the Dreaming Room LLC, Certified Capital Advisors, the Entrepreneur Capital Cooperation, and the Michael E. Gerber Club.

ALSO BY MICHAEL GERBER

Awakening the Entrepreneur Within,
The E-Myth Revisited,
and
E-Myth Mastery

THE E-MYTH
ENTERPRISE

How to Turn a Great Idea
into a Thriving Business

MICHAEL E. GERBER

HARPER
BUSINESS

HARPER

BUSINESS

THE E-MYTH ENTERPRISE. Copyright © 2009 by Michael Gerber. All rights reserved. Printed in the United States of America. No part of this book may be used or reproduced in any manner whatsoever without written permission except in the case of brief quotations embodied in critical articles and reviews. For information, address HarperCollins Publishers, 10 East 53rd Street, New York, NY 10022.

HarperCollins books may be purchased for educational, business, or sales promotional use. For information please write: Special Markets Department, HarperCollins Publishers, 10 East 53rd Street, New York, NY 10022.

A hardcover edition of this book was published in 2009 by Harper Business.

FIRST HARPER BUSINESS PAPERBACK EDITION PUBLISHED 2010.

Library of Congress Cataloging-in-Publication data is available upon request.

ISBN 978-0-06-173382-6 (pbk.)

10 11 12 13 14   OV/RRD 10 9 8 7 6 5 4 3 2 1

To the Dreamers who bravely take action.

ACKNOWLEDGMENTS

Of course, no book is born without inspiration, education, and dog-dirty help:

To my new-found team at COLLINS, including my publisher, Hollis Heimbouch, my senior editor and nurse, Ben Steinberg, and the strong and dedicated production team, Helen Song (don't you just love that name?), Nicolette Cutler, William Ruoto, and Elliott Beard, thank you all.

To my great new friend and workhorse editor, Steven Gottry, where would I be without you?

To my friend for all seasons and committed (at times reluctant) agent and cautioneer, Steven Hanselman, we've got a lot more left to do so no resting on your laurels.

To my expansive, dedicated, cherished and cherishing wife, Luz Delia, this is the second one you've seen me through.

To Ken Blanchard who has now written forewords to

my last two books, but is not, himself, too forward at all, thank you Ken for your care and passionate interest in me and all things entrepreneurial.

To my readers by the millions and to my associates in all my various ventures, including E-Myth Worldwide, In The Dreaming Room, Chief Dreamer Enterprises, Club Entrepreneur Network, The Entrepreneur Capital Corporation, Biz-Dog.com, The Michael Gerber Club, and many, many more, thank you all for your zealous commitment to the outcome we all crave—the transformation of small business worldwide.

And to you, dear reader, if you've gotten this far . . . this is all about you and what you hope to do . . . how could it be any other way?

CONTENTS

FOREWORD

I love to read Michael Gerber's books. His attitude is challenging, his style is playful, and his content is insightful. His early gems—*The E-Myth, E-Myth Mastery, The E-Myth Revisited,* and *Awakening the Entrepreneur Within*—were pretty darn good, to say the least. But *The E-Myth Enterprise* might be his best book yet. Listen to what Michael has to say in his introduction:

> Trust me when I say this: The E-Myth Enterprises you will come in touch with here are as uncommon a reality as winning the Olympics. . . . Companies like these don't just happen; They are the outcome of passions intensely applied. Of perseverance impossible to fake. Of overcoming the relentless obstacles that are continually conspiring to make the impossible, impossible. To make the unfathomable, unfathomable. To make the difficult more than just

difficult, but horrendously difficult. Of creating an original result in the world. . . . In short, a free market system provides one with significantly more opportunity to fail than it does to succeed.

How's that for challenging? He points out later in the book:

Service is an incomplete word because it says, "The customer is king." But as it works out in real life, the customer isn't king except in the mind of the customer. To the employees, the customer isn't king; he's often a pain in the ass. To suppliers, the customer isn't queen; she's often a problem waiting to happen. To the lenders, the customer isn't king; he's often a drunk hanging on to a wagon, caroming into a wall. No, the customer isn't king to them—they are!

How's that for playful? Throughout the book, Michael gets to the heart of what makes businesses tick:

There are three things that can be organized: time, space, and work. Despite what many believe—and what most try to do—people cannot be organized. Only the work people do can be organized. All attempts to organize people instead of their work do exactly the opposite of what organization is intended to do. Rather than order, it creates chaos. Rather than ease, it creates dis-ease. Rather than efficiency, it creates boredom. Rather than flexibility, it creates bureaucracy. Rather than room, it creates confinement . . . When employed with skill, organization always produces a sense of great ease. When employed unwisely, organization always produces resistance. *I have never seen a great business that does things in a businesslike way.*

How's that for insightful?

Is *The E-Myth Enterprise* just for people thinking about starting a business? No, but it sure would help. I read this book on a plane from Dallas to San Diego. After finishing a page, I would hand it to my wife, Margie, who cofounded our company with me and who has, by the way, a PhD in communication. She kept saying as she read, "How do we get everyone in our company to read this book?" We're celebrating the thirtieth anniversary of our company this year and Margie is worried that we have what is called "educational incapacity." Our success—and we have been successful—makes us blind to new learnings and ways of thinking. And boy, is *The E-Myth Enterprise* all about that.

So read this book. Share it with your colleagues. And, as Michael Gerber challenges us, "Stop sleeping! Wake up!" Heed the final thoughts in this wonderful book by this brilliant, passionate man, Michael Gerber, who I am proud to call a new friend.

A business with conscience.

That is, I believe, the only mission worthy of the name.

To create a world in which people are present, honest, open, and alive.

To create a world in which people make conscious decisions in good conscience.

That is what shooting for the moon is all about.

And one cannot do it in one's sleep.

It requires all we have.

And it requires *now*.

> — Ken Blanchard, coauthor of *The One Minute Manager*®
> and *The One Minute Entrepreneur*™ and cofounder
> and Chief Spiritual Officer of The Ken Blanchard Companies

PREFACE

HOW PIG AND BEAR WENT INTO BUSINESS

Pig and Bear decided to go into business.

"We'll make lots of money!" they thought.

Pig baked a bushel of potatoes, and Bear fried a heap of doughnuts.

They went to the marketplace early in the morning to get the best spots. Nobody was around yet. The morning was clear and chilly. Bear had a nickel in his coat. After a while he went over to Pig's stand to warm up a little.

"How much for a potato?" he growled.

"A nickel for you."

Bear was about to say that he'd just wanted to ask, but then he changed his mind. He fished for the nickel in his fur, took the biggest steaming potato in his paws, and crossed the road back to his stand.

The business is moving, rejoiced Pig. But since there were no more customers for a while, and he hadn't eaten since they started at dawn, he crossed over to Bear's stand and bought himself a black raspberry doughnut for a nickel.

Bear was happy to have his first customer. He felt he should eat something before they started to flock. He went over to buy another baked potato. The move brought him luck. He had hardly finished when Pig was over for another doughnut.

The business slacked off again until Bear bought a potato. Soon Pig was over again, and Bear went right back to his stand with him to spend the earned nickel. Pig returned for a doughnut, and soon they were going back and forth until they sold everything.

They counted the money, but:

"How strange, I only have a nickel," Bear said.

"And I have nothing at all," said Pig.

They couldn't believe it.

"We have sold all our merchandise," they kept saying, "but we have no money!"

But in vain they counted and recounted: they had only a nickel between them after the whole day of busy trading.

—Adapted from *Twelve Iron Sandals* by Vit Hořejš

INTRODUCTION

If you've read any of my *E-Myth* books, you know me well enough to anticipate what I'm about to share with you. If you haven't read my *E-Myth* books, this book will come as a surprise.

The E-Myth Enterprise is a book about the business of invention. More importantly, it's a book about rare people who I have come to think of as true E-Myth Entrepreneurs, people who were moved to re-create their world by inventing a business unlike any they had ever seen other than in their imagination.

Unlike any business *you* have ever seen.

Trust me when I say this: the E-Myth Enterprises you will come in touch with here are as uncommon a reality as winning the Olympics.

Companies like these don't simply happen; they are the product of deep, delirious imagining. They are the outcome of passions intensely applied. Of perseverance impossible to fake. Of overcoming the relentless obstacles that are continually conspiring to make the impossible impossible. To make the unfathomable unfathomable. To make the difficult more than just difficult, but horrendously difficult. Of creating an original result in the world.

I think you get what I mean. Don't try this at home, is what the warning reads at the bottom of the page. Unless you're determined to exceed, that is.

To exceed what? is the question.

Well, of course: to exceed the everyday. The normal. The obvious.

And if that's the case, this book tells you what it looks like when you're done and how to think about it in the process.

How to invent an E-Myth Enterprise.

How to invent a company that acts like one in ten million.

Welcome to the club. The E-Myth Club. The Michael Gerber Club. The club of great entrepreneurs.

THE FOUR ESSENTIAL INGREDIENTS

I was having a conversation with my friend and agent, Steve Hanselman, not that long ago, about my commitment to create a new master's degree, one that would leave an MBA and all those who would pursue it smothered in the dust.

I called that new degree an MBD, or master's of business design.

It would be the only business program an entrepreneur or an entrepreneurial manager would ever need. It would teach the essential skills needed to invent a stunningly original company, what I in this book call an E-Myth Enterprise.

There are four essential ingredients to building such a company: they are the visual, emotional, functional, and financial. When you design a company, you design it visually, emotionally, functionally, and financially. These four essential components call for a systems thinker if they are to be designed to work as all great companies work: synergistically, in an integrated, intelligent, original, emotionally compelling way to deliver the original promise they were designed to deliver, a result that surprises the people it was intended to surprise, that glues them to it in ways they had never expected because it serves them in ways they had never expected. And it keeps on doing it because it was built in a very special way.

In this book I will discuss the beginnings of that MBD, at least to the point where you will clearly understand the logic underlying it and why it is so critical for you should you aspire to become such an inventor, such an E-Myth Entrepreneur, as the folks in this book have become.

The idea is not that difficult to grasp. A company is a product of an entrepreneur's imagination. It is a visual product, an emotional product, a functional product, and a financial product.

Although the idea is not that difficult, it seems that most people I tell that to do find it difficult and, for many, impossible to get. I believe that to be caused by the gross, commercial, flat, unstimulating, unimaginative context most of us hold on to when relating to the subject of business.

Business, to most people, is what their parents did or do.

Business, to most people, is the job they've got to go to today.

Business, to most people, is where we work.

Business, to most people, is where we would least like to be if what we really wanted to be doing is having fun.

This book suggests something significantly different than that.

Business is the most creative and challenging pursuit in which one can engage. It is also downright fun—if done right.

Follow me. Let's do it right! Let's have fun!

—Michael Gerber

THE E-MYTH
ENTERPRISE

CHAPTER ONE

THE E-MYTH ENTERPRISE AND THE POSITION OF ONE: A BUSINESS EXISTS ONLY AS IT IS PERCEIVED BY OTHERS

■

> In too many situations
> we automatically
> experience people
> as "them"—not "us."
> These jungle-type
> habits of mind
> are dangerous
> to our species.
>
> —Ken Keyes Jr.

This book is meant to be a prescription for building a successful business in a free market system. As you will find out, it probably serves as well—if not better—as a polemic against such prescriptions.

Please excuse the apparent contradiction. I know that if you're patient, somewhere in the middle resides a truth worth digging for. But to get there, you're going to have to do some of the work. You're going to have to stretch where I stretch and let go where I let go.

In other words, you're going to have to be willing to play an always frustrating, but sometimes enlightening, game, a game I call how do you provide an answer to a question that you know has no answer?

In a free market system, that's the game called business.

To anyone with even a passing interest in the comings and goings of the free market system in the United States, it should be apparent that the life of a business here is a precarious thing. If the business is a good idea—that is, if it does all the right things in the right way and at the right time, and is lucky—it succeeds.

If it's a bad idea, it doesn't.

Even worse, it could appear to be a good idea, but shifts—more like earthquakes—in the economy can sink it. Wasn't Washington Mutual a good idea? Wasn't Fannie Mae? Wasn't Lehman Brothers? Wasn't AIG?

Unfortunately, the truth is that for the people who invest in other people's businesses, for those who start a business of their own, or for those who work for either of the other two, most businesses turn out to be bad ideas; most businesses fail. Even the so-called giants.

More frustrating is that, in a free market system, even

the good ideas—the businesses that succeed—turn into the bad ideas in time.

The weather changes. A new company moves in across the street. People stop having babies. Somebody comes up with a better idea. The economy experiences a so-called correction. Or—and this happens—someone comes up with a worse idea but implements it better.

In short, a free market system provides all of us with significantly more opportunity to fail than to succeed.

What worked yesterday will most likely not work today, and the fact that something works today is insufficient justification for planning to do it the same way tomorrow.

How can we minimize the risk?

If an estimated six out of ten companies funded by professional venture capitalists go under (some estimates run as high as 90 percent*), how can anyone else expect to do better? Shouldn't we be able to expect better in a world with so much information at hand, with so much technical and technological know-how at our disposal, and with so many well-trained managers available?

For years, clients have been asking me those very questions.

Is there a common denominator we can use to take a more accurate measure of a business idea?

Is there a pattern—a template—we can use to evalu-

---

* http://www.smallbusiness.com/wiki/Venture_capital.

ate a business and its likelihood of achieving significant success?

Is there something all great businesses do that can be replicated by other businesses wishing to become great?

Is there a way to clone greatness?

I believe the answer to each of these questions is yes.

This book is my answer to those thousands of clients and businesspeople who have asked me these questions over the years, as well as to the millions of entrepreneurs, would-be entrepreneurs, and managers I have never met to whom these questions are just as important.

In a deceptively thin book, I have organized the fundamental principles that I believe form the foundation of every lasting great business into a template or model of greatness, the presence of which in any business would indicate with a great degree of certainty what I call the *success-proneness* of that business, and the absence of which would indicate that a business is not likely to pass the test of time.

The value of this template is that it is timeless. It will work for any enterprise, any time, at any place in the world.

It transcends epochs, technology, industry, markets, economies, and geography.

It could have been implemented as effectively in the nineteenth century as it is now.

It could be put to good work just as effectively in the emerging Eastern European free market experiment, as it could in the United States free market's attempt to recapture its own lost glory.

It could just as well be applied to a corner grocery store as to a semiconductor plant in Chandler, Arizona, or an iPod factory in China.

The reason it is so timeless and so transferable is because it is founded upon the one sacrosanct requirement upon which the existence of every business in a free market system always has depended, and always will depend.

That is, to succeed, every business in a free market system must learn how to satisfy, better than its competitors, the essential needs, unconscious expectations, and perceived preferences of the four most important groups of people in its universe: (1) the people who work for it; (2) the people who buy from it; (3) the people who sell to it; and (4) the people who lend to it: its employees, customers, suppliers, and financial institutions.

It is the combined judgment of all these people, these four primary influencers, upon which the ultimate success or failure—yes, the life or death—of every business enterprise ultimately depends.

Which brings us to our first rule of thumb.

And that is, in a free market system . . .

Businesses Exist Only Because People Want Them To.

I hope that statement doesn't come as a big surprise to you.

It surprises me that most businesses seem to operate as though exactly the opposite were true.

As though people exist *because* of businesses.

As though God created businesses first, and only when the businesses were seen not to work did He create people to go to work in them, to buy from them, to sell to them, and to lend to them.

I know that's a dumb thing to say—I know it.

But it's an even dumber thing to *do*. Yet for many businesses it's standard operating procedure.

Which brings us to our second rule of thumb. And that is, in a free market system . . .

People Are Regarded as a Problem to Most Businesses.

Yes, to most businesses in a free market system, people are regarded as a problem—not only the people who work in the business, but the people who sell to the business, the people who buy from the business, and the people who lend to the business. All people are regarded as a problem. And they're a problem because they're so *unmanageable*. When people are manageable, they're not a problem anymore. They're invisible.

That's what most businesses I have seen would like

people to be. Invisible. Not a problem. Not needing attention. Pliable. *Easy.*

That's why there are systems in the world other than the free market system.

Other systems were created to eliminate the problem of people. In other systems, people aren't a problem because it doesn't matter what they want.

In a free market system, you can't get away with that mind-set for very long, and that's what drives everybody nuts trying to run a business in this system.

In a free market system, we have to come to grips with the fact that there are all these people—needing, needing, needing.

Unfortunately, in a free market system, all of them are needing the same damn thing—MORE!

More of what?
More of everything!
But don't people know that there's only so much a business can give?
Why aren't they understanding, like us?
Like who?

Like businesspeople.
Like the people who run the business.
Like the people here in the business at the top.
Like the people who own the business.
Like the people who manage the business.

Like the people who would like other people to be
more reasonable.
Like the people very much like us, who want . . .
what?

Who want MORE.
Who want more of what?
Of everything!
But a business can only give so much!
Who said?

* * *

In a free market system, businesses are invented by people
for a very special reason.

But despite what most of us believe, businesses are not
invented only by those people who go into business—the
so-called entrepreneurs among us.

In a free market system, businesses are invented by
all of us—by each and every one of us. The reason we
invent businesses in a free market system, like ours in
the United States, is to do one thing—and only one
thing: to create MORE. Businesses in a free market
system are the instruments through which people get
MORE.

In all other systems, businesses are the instrument
through which most people hopefully get *enough* (but

rarely do), while some people—some very few people—get the MORE that everyone else isn't getting.

But in the free market system, *everyone* is supposed to get MORE.

The problem with the free market system is that when everyone doesn't get the MORE that they want, then "shit happens" (as the crude bumper sticker states).

And that's the part of the free market system called *business,* which very few people in business seem to fully understand.

A business in the free market system is only justifiable in the minds of people—is only tolerated in the minds of people, *is only permitted to exist in the minds of people*—if the business learns how to give them MORE.

A business is intended to be a perpetual motion machine, the only purpose of which is to find ways to give people MORE.

A business is a mechanism designed to produce MORE for the continually rising expectations of people in a free market system.

And in a free market system, the minute a business forgets these things, the minute a business stops providing MORE, the minute a business begins to ignore its sole purpose for being in a free market system—its raison d'être—it ceases playing the game called business.

It begins to play the game called *good-bye.*

Which brings us to our third rule of thumb.

And that is, in a free market system . . .

Service Is an Incomplete Word.

If everyone understood that, in a free market system such as we have in the United States, the game called business is all about creating MORE for everyone, we would immediately understand why *service* is an incomplete word: it doesn't include enough.

It doesn't include the employees. It doesn't include the suppliers. It doesn't include the lenders. It only includes the customers.

Service is an incomplete word because it says, "The customer is king!"

But as it works out in real life, the customer *isn't* king except in the mind of the customer.

To the employees, the customer isn't king; he's often a pain in the ass.

To the suppliers, the customer isn't queen; she's often a problem waiting to happen.

To the lenders, the customer isn't king; he's often a drunk hanging on to a wagon careening into a wall.

No, the customer isn't king to them—*they* are!

"If the customer is king," they all ask privately, deep in the hidden recesses of their longing hearts, "what about *me*?"

That's what everybody else is asking too: "What about me?"

That's what happens when we don't understand the game of business as it's meant to be played in a free market system. People start asking the most obvious questions.

It should be obvious that, by itself, a strong focus on the customer is insufficient to create a successful business. There can be no such thing as effective customer service in a company where the employees are disenchanted, where the owners aren't making a decent profit, where the suppliers aren't getting paid on time.

In short, a strong focus on customer service not only is insufficient to produce lasting results in a company, but, in itself, makes lasting results impossible to achieve.

Which brings us to our fourth rule of thumb.

And that is, in a free market system . . . .

There Aren't Any Good Answers for Long.

If, as we've already agreed, the purpose of a business is to serve as an instrument through which people in a free market system get what they want—and what they always want is MORE—then it is safe to assume that any business that comes up with MORE is serving its purpose well, and therefore survives. Any business that fails to come up with MORE is not serving its purpose at all, and therefore dies.

This leads us to the unavoidable conclusion that every

time a business comes up with an answer, that answer bears within it the seeds of its own demise.

Every answer in a successful business is only a temporary solution reached on the never-ending path toward the search for MORE.

Which means that for businesses operating in the Land of MORE, there aren't any answers, only questions. And the questions all lead in the same direction—the direction that every sensible, aware, responsive, dynamic chief executive officer knows as the only way to MORE.

This is the way every successful business operating in a free market system from time immemorial has followed: the search for the ineffable, the indefinable, the unknowable, the indisputably, irrefutably, pragmatically, unavoidably aggravating Holy Grail of MORE.

The only justification necessary is "If *we* don't, they will. And if they find it first, our ass is grass."

Which leads us to our fifth rule of thumb.

And that is, in a free market system . . .

You Are Either the Lawn Mower or the Lawn.

Which is where we began this little moralistic tale—that in a free market system, business is a precarious thing; your very *survival* is at stake.

And in the Land of MORE, as we've already learned, if you don't survive, it's because you didn't *deserve* to.

You weren't paying attention.
Somebody opened the gate and rolled in the John
Deere while you weren't looking.
Suddenly, your role was defined for you: your ass
was grass.

This is the same way the role is defined for most businesses, every single day of the year: because they aren't playing the game called business; they're playing the game called good-bye.

What's sad is that they refuse to accept that there's a difference between the two games.

Yes, it's sad and it's true that most businesses, large and small, are living by rules of thumb that aren't rules at all, but the cover of the box they've laid down in.

They have stopped asking questions and have come up with an unsuitable (that is, self-serving) answer.

A close friend of mine wrote a book about the meaning of money. He observed that few of us really understand what money is; we simply use it. He feels strongly that we're paying a big price for our ignorance.

I feel the same way about business.

Like money, business touches each and every one of us at every turn—our food, our clothes, our entertainment, our recreation, our health—our very life. Every choice we make is impacted by business in some form, creating some service or product upon which we depend, or have grown to depend, if not for our very survival, at least for the survival of the lifestyle we have grown to enjoy.

Every day, all around us, businesses are being born, living, struggling, and dying. Each of them, like each of us, is a unique being with a unique identity and a unique place in the world. All of the characteristics found in each of us—active or passive, creative or dull, passionate or stingy, growing or withdrawn—can be found in a business.

Yet, just as with money, few of us understand what this thing called business really is. We go to work in them, buy from them, and have opinions about them. But we don't understand them.

To most people, business is what goes on around us while we get on with our lives, something being done "out there"—at most a commercial enterprise, a place to make money, a place to go to work, a place to buy things, or a place that makes things we buy.

Few people seem to understand that business is much more than these individual factors.

In a free market system, business isn't what goes on around us while we get on with our lives. Business *is* our lives.

Business is what we do, all we do, who we *are*.

In a free market system, business is the organized expression of our growing self-interest manifesting itself the best way it knows how.

Business is a living thing.

Look at our businesses, and you'll know who we are.

In a free market system, everyone is touched by the allure of business. You can't get away from it.

Writers talk about the business of writing books.
Artists talk about the business of creating art.
Intellectuals talk about the business of communi-
cating ideas.
Spiritualists talk about the business of raising our
spiritual awareness.
Meditators talk about the business of teaching us
how to sit.
Chiropractors talk about the business of teaching
us how to stand.
Preachers are in the religion business.
Musicians are in the music business.
Pediatricians are in the baby business.
Cardiologists are in the heart business.

We have taken the world apart and put it back together again as a business.

The business of government.
The business of education.
The business of health.
The business of art.

We live the illusion that we understand what business is, when in fact we don't.

Despite what most people think, business isn't doing or creating something to be sold.

Business is a living thing that feeds and grows on the expectations, perceptions, needs, fears, and greed of the people with whom it comes into contact.

Business is a product of everything we believe to be true, need to be true, want to be true.

Our businesses are us, and we are our businesses.

Which brings us to the point at hand: the E-Myth Enterprise and the Position of One.

That is, a business, any business, can succeed only to the degree that it gives each and every one of its four primary influencers MORE than they can expect from any one of its competitors.

The way in which a business accomplishes this objective is what we would call a *good idea*.

An idea that will attract customers to it.
An idea that will attract employees to it.
An idea that will attract suppliers to it.
An idea that will attract lenders to it.

It is an idea that attracts, with the greatest of force, the interest and attention of the four primary influencers, and acts with the same force with which it attracts.

The force of any idea originates in the essential needs, perceived preferences, and unconscious expectations of the people it is intended to serve; an idea has no force of its own.

Thought of in that way, a good idea for a business is one that serves the most people best. A bad idea for a business is one that serves the most people least.

The Position of One is that locus of energy—that fusion of attention—created when a good idea attracts to itself the self-interests of customers, employees, suppliers, and lenders alike with an equal, active, intensely interested force, which then moves out into the world to attract more force, which, in turn, moves out into the world to attract even more force, thus growing and expanding and exploding with a power unrivaled by its competitors.

Like a star. Like the sun. Like the eye of a storm.

That's the power of the Position of One.

* * *

DESIGNING THE ENTERPRISE:
THE TAKEAWAY POINTS

**(Listen to the Podcast version
at MichaelEGerber.com)**

■

My brief summaries will end every chapter and include the essential ideas that you need to post on your wall, burn into your brain, think about during your commute, and remember every day—as you build your E-Myth Enterprise. Go to MichaelEGerber.com for my Podcast—and new information that will impact your enterprise in even greater ways.

- **Businesses exist only because people want them to.** We want businesses to serve our needs. Fulfill our desires. Make our lives better. More, more, more! When they fail to do that—or no longer succeed as they once did—do we still want them to exist? How will your customers feel about your business next year? In five years? In ten years?
- **People are regarded as a problem to most businesses.** The shake-ups in the financial sector clearly illustrate the failure of leaders, systems,

and consumer protections. We all recognize that we want—and need—banks and investment firms. But we want them to function properly. To keep our money safe. To remain solvent. To be managed and staffed by people who place our interests first. E-Myth Enterprises reduce and resolve problems, refine the "people selection process."

- **_Service_ is an incomplete word.** The customer cannot be king if management is king. The customer cannot be king if employees are king. In an E-Myth Enterprise, owners, managers, employees, suppliers, and lenders must come into alignment and crown the customer. _Service_ then becomes a complete word.

- **There aren't any good answers for long.** Customers want More, More, More. Obviously, you can't offer Less, Less, Less. Changing needs and wants MUST change the way you do business.

- **The E-Myth Enterprise and the Position of One.** Any business can succeed only if it gives its four primary influencers MORE than they can expect from a competitor. This is accomplished through a good idea that will attract customers, employees, suppliers, and lenders to it.

* * *

CHAPTER TWO

THE E-MYTH ENTREPRENEUR
AND THE FIVE ESSENTIAL SKILLS

■

**The real unknown
is an emotional
unknown. . . .
We awaken to
darkness.**

—Jacob Needleman

If a good idea for a business is one that serves the most people best, then we in the United States have some soul searching to do, because there's something missing in most of our businesses. And that something is *meaning*.

For our failure to understand the true role business has come to play in our lives, for our failure to truly listen to the people we come into contact with, for our bias toward serving our own special interests, for our raw, insatiable drive to get the material MORE we all seem to be saying we need, it can't be denied that too many of our businesses have become killing fields of the spirit. They, like us, have missed the deeper message.

To truly soar—especially if the economy is challenging—a business must mean more than just money, more than just "things," more than what's easy, more than careers, inventory, production statistics, ROI, automobiles, lip gloss, remodeled kitchens, management by objectives, pensions, profit sharing, "golden parachutes," and current trends and fashions.

To achieve some measure of greatness, a business must somehow rise above the one-dimensional symbols and empty rituals of our everyday flat-world existence.

To truly attract the greatest amount of force and the greatest attention—to fully seize its potential power—the idea behind a business must strike much deeper.

It must strike our imagination.

It must touch a strong, resonant, and resilient chord in the hearts of all those people it is intended to serve.

It must use its energy in a profound, intelligent, and compassionate way.

It must reach beyond the trivial, the course, the ordinary, the mundane.

It must give us more life.

It must become a presence impossible to ignore.

It must become a place in which the most transient
MORE, the most predictable MORE, the most
superficial MORE, the most immediate MORE,
the most trivial MORE is never enough.

It must become heroic in everything it does.

It must touch the dying part of each and every
one of us and raise us to some higher place.

Five essential skills are needed at the outset to create
a great business. I say at the outset, for these skills must
be in place if the idea for the business is to possess the
size, the scale, the magnitude, the ecstatic quality—the
power—needed to enter the race.

To some degree, every great business possesses these
skills. I would go so far as to say that a business without
them is dead.

■

**The first essential skill—the most
fundamental of all—is *concentration*.**

Concentration is the foundation upon which all right
action in the world depends.

Without concentration, a business will have no presence, no inner force, no magnetic center to which people,
upon whom it depends for its life, energy, and force, will

be attracted. Without concentration, there is no ability to listen, to respond, to be available.

Concentration is not only something a great business must do, it is also the result of such doing. As a business concentrates its attention, it also becomes concentrated—the convergent point to which energy is drawn.

The t'ai chi master T'an Meng-hsien, in his *Song of Central Equilibrium*, says:

> *We are centered, stable and still*
> *as a mountain*
> *Our ch'i sinks to the tan-t'ien and*
> *we are as if suspended from above.*
> *Our spirit is concentrated within and*
> *our outward manner perfectly composed.*
> *Receiving and issuing energy are*
> *both the work of an instant.*

Said another way, a great business owns a place in the world.

> It stands squarely in that place but is able to move
>   in an instant.
> Its energy, its *ch'i,* flows without obstruction.
> It is loose, flexible, yet as solid as a mountain.
> Its face looks within and without in the very same
>   moment.

Its power is continuously in motion yet, at the
same time, infinitely still.
All are drawn to it as to a vision.
It does important things.

In today's world, I think of Apple. While this company
owns only a small share of the personal computer market
(the most recent number I heard was 8 percent), it stands
in a place in the world that is indisputable. It owns the
MP3 domain, as well as the music download realm. Others
want that market. Microsoft wants to torpedo Apple with
the Zune. But the energy of Steve Jobs and his team is
planted solidly on a vision to do important things.

By the time you read this, Apple could be gone. It
almost disappeared in 1993, when Jobs was not a part
of the picture. But my guess is that Apple's energy will
continue to flow without obstruction. It will be the company of MORE, offering more in its iPods, its iPhones,
and its computers, all of which continue to be cutting
edge. That's the focus; that's where concentration meets
MORE.

■

**The second essential skill is
discrimination, the ability to choose upon
what, where, and whom our attention, our
ability to concentrate, is directed.**

If concentration provides us with the attention and energy we need, discrimination provides us with the intention, the will to select the most important work to do.

> It is through discrimination that a business develops standards, both strategically, in the form of a mission, and tactically, in the form of behavior.
> It is through the development of standards that a business develops discipline.
> It is through the development of discipline that a business develops patience.
> It is through the development of patience that a business develops vision.
> It is through the development of vision that a business develops insight.
> It is through the development of insight that a business develops conviction.
> It is through the development of conviction that a business develops awareness.
> It is through the development of awareness that a business develops empathy.

It is through the development of empathy that a
business develops relationships.
It is through the development of relationships that
a business develops more life.

Again, Apple provides a stunning example of this
thread leading from discrimination to conviction, to
awareness, to empathy, to relationships, to life. This is
what explains the phenomenon of "Mac Evangelists,"
those die-hard loyalists who would stand in line for hours,
if not days, to buy the latest model iPhone, even if it were
made out of recycled cardboard. Apple understands that
discrimination, the ability to choose upon what, where,
and whom its attention, its ability to concentrate, is directed, ultimately leads to relationships—and that develops more life.

■

**The third essential skill is *organization*,
the ability to turn chaos into order.**

If concentration provides the energy and attention needed
for right action to take place, and discrimination provides the intention and standards needed to know what
action needs to be taken, then organization provides the
room for right action to take place.

■

There are three things that can be so organized: time, space, and work.

(Despite what many believe—and what most try to do— people cannot be organized. Only the work people do can be organized. All attempts to organize people instead of their work create exactly the opposite of what organization is intended to do. Rather than order, it creates chaos. Rather than ease, it creates dis-ease. Rather than efficiency, it creates boredom. Rather than flexibility, it creates bureaucracy. Rather than room, it creates confinement.)

The *organization of time* prevents the overutilization of energy to achieve one's objectives; just enough time— and no more—within which the right action can be efficiently performed.

The *organization of space* produces the right tools in the right place in the right quantity to support the right action with an economy of effort.

The *organization of work* identifies the natural way to take action, the relationships between functions, and the coordination between the two.

When employed with skill, organization always produces a sense of great ease.

When employed unwisely, organization always produces resistance.

I believe that Starbucks is a stunning—yet simple—example of organization at work. The typical Starbucks, especially in places such as downtown Manhattan, can have, at times, long lines that stretch out the doors and onto the sidewalks. This could easily translate into chaos. But it usually doesn't. Time is organized because someone is approaching customers at the end of the line and "walky-talky-ing" the order to the cashier, who relays it to the barista. The space and the tools are organized to enable the efficient and timely delivery of drinks. And everything is coordinated beautifully, from the order taker, to the cashier, to the barista, to the delivery of the drink. Of course, not every Starbucks experience is perfect, but it's clear that the organization of time, space, and work is a serious goal.

■

The fourth essential skill, *innovation*, turns order into right action.

Innovation is sometimes called the "Best Way" skill; it is always in search of perfection.

While organization is interested in efficiency, innovation is concerned with effectiveness—faster, cheaper, smoother, softer.

Innovation is what children do all the time. Like children, it is playful, bright, light, and joyful.

Also like children, innovation is almost always irresponsible. Left to its own devices, it will almost always get itself in trouble.

It is always imagining new possibilities and acting on such imagining.

It is willing to try anything once.

That is why without concentration, discrimination, and organization, innovation could very well sink the ship.

On the other hand, without innovation, the ship wouldn't be very much fun.

Again, I turn to the example of Apple. Imagine walking into a retail technology store with your offspring in tow, and while you're devising ways to spend possibly thousands of dollars on gadgets, your kid gets to sit down on kid-sized chairs in front of a kid-sized table filled with kid-friendly computers to play kid-type games—while you shop for adult-friendly toys. That's Apple. That's innovation. Hands-on innovation. Not cheaper, but certainly smoother and softer.

■

The fifth essential skill is *communication*.

It is the skill through which results are produced in the

world. Shamefully, they're not always the good, desirable results for which we hope and pray. Sometimes they're the opposite.

But communication touches and is touched, reaches out and is reached for, moves and is moved upon, acts and is acted upon.

Communication is the channel through which life is conveyed, through which the energy of the idea is transmitted, through which the mind and the body and the spirit are merged and projected into a force for right action.

It is the medium through which attractions are formed, then deepen.

It is the bond we each have with the world.

All of the great leaders in history have been great communicators. Abraham Lincoln. Winston Churchill. John F. Kennedy. Martin Luther King, Jr. Ronald Reagan. Some you may admire, some you may not. And then there's Adolf Hitler. Not a force for right action. Certainly not on anyone's list of most admired, but an effective communicator, nonetheless. He's the opposite that I mentioned.

* * *

DESIGNING THE ENTERPRISE: THE TAKEAWAY POINTS

**(Listen to the Podcast version
at MichaelEGerber.com)**

■

The E-Myth Enterprise is created and led by an individual who possesses five essential skills. Having only two, three, or even four of these skills will lead to certain disaster.

- **The first essential skill—the most fundamental of all—is concentration.**

    Without concentration, a business will be ordinary in every respect, because it will have no presence, no inner force, no way to attract the people upon whom it depends for its life, energy, and force—employees, customers, suppliers, and lenders. Without concentration, there is no ability to listen, to respond, to be available to the four primary influencers.

- **The second essential skill is discrimination, the ability to choose upon what, where, and whom our attention, our ability to concentrate, is directed.**

    Business owners who do not have the skill of

discrimination tend to believe that everything is of equal importance. They overlook the significant in favor of the urgent. That which is happening around them captures their attention. Bob Jones, Sr. once advised, "Never sacrifice the permanent on the altar of the immediate." •

■ **The third essential skill is organization, the ability to turn chaos into order.**

There are three things that can be so organized: time, space, and work.

The organization of time prevents the overutilization of energy to achieve one's objectives; just enough time—and no more—within which the right action can be efficiently performed.

The organization of space produces the right tools in the right place in the right quantity to support the right action with an economy of effort.

The organization of work identifies the natural way to take action, the relationships between functions, and the coordination between the two.

■ **The fourth essential skill, innovation, turns order into right action.** Innovation is sometimes called the "Best Way" skill; it is always in search of perfection.

While organization is interested in efficiency, innovation is concerned with effectiveness— faster, cheaper, smoother, softer.

▪ **The fifth essential skill is communication.** It is the skill through which results are produced in the world. Communication touches and is touched, reaches out and is reached for, moves and is moved upon, acts and is acted upon.

* * *

CHAPTER THREE

THE E-MYTH ENTERPRISE MATRIX: THE FOUR CATEGORIES OF PREFERENCE

∎

The constituents of matter and the basic phenomena involving them are all interconnected, interrelated, and interdependent. . . . They cannot be understood as isolated entities, but only as integrated parts of the whole.

—Fritjof Capra, *The Tao of Physics*

On my sixteenth birthday, many years ago, I bought a very special car. It was a 1947 Ford coupe.

I think of John Anderson, the man who sold it to me, as the quintessential entrepreneur.

Not that I thought of him like that at the time.

At the time I wasn't interested in business. I was simply a sixteen-year-old boy who was about to negotiate the most important decision of his life, and John Anderson was the man who was either going to make it possible or not.

In retrospect, I know that John Anderson was a business genius. Whether by intention or not, he did every little thing right.

A few words about John Anderson.

He wasn't in business at all, but an engineer working at Lockheed.

I saw his small classified ad in the *Anaheim Bulletin,* announcing the fact that he had a 1947 Ford for sale.

The ad said, mysteriously: "Once you see it, you'll wonder why."

I called, scheduled an appointment for the following day after school, then proceeded to climb the walls for twenty-four hours until the time came to see the car.

What I had failed to tell John Anderson over the phone was the fact that I had three seemingly insurmountable problems.

One, I hadn't told my folks that I was going to buy a car.

Two, I didn't have enough money to buy a car.

And, three, I absolutely couldn't live for another day without owning my own car!

It was with that knowledge festering inside of me that I nervously rang John Anderson's doorbell that Thursday afternoon.

John Anderson opened the door.

He was a slim, tall, nondescript man with neatly cropped blond hair and bright blue, intelligent-looking eyes. He was in his early forties, although he looked much younger.

He was wearing a khaki shirt, open at the collar, and matching trousers. Both were starched and pressed with a military crispness.

His brown shoes gleamed.

He smiled warmly, shook my hand, invited me in, introduced me to his wife, who was shelling peas at the kitchen table, then led me out to the garage, where he told me he kept the car.

The small, white, single-car garage stood separately from the house. I followed John Anderson to the garage door and waited for what seemed like an eternity while he unlocked a large padlock secured to the door handle.

As though anticipating the question I didn't have the nerve to ask, he said: "I keep the door locked, just in case."

In case of what, I couldn't imagine. Until he opened the door.

Standing before us was the car, completely enclosed in a tight-fitting canvas tarp. The sole object in the garage, it sat frozen—as though hovering—in the space before me. It was a surprise package waiting to be opened, a mystery waiting to be revealed.

It was as if John Anderson had brought me to his garage to unveil a secret he had been hiding there for who knows how long—one he was about to share for the very first time, with me, and only me, his unwitting coconspirator. It was almost more than I could bear.

"Would you like to help me take this off?" he asked as he moved to the front of the car, touching the canvas tarp lightly with his hand.

Was he kidding?

I mumbled something incoherent like, "Mmhmm," then waited for the instructions I knew would come. Instinctively I knew you didn't simply grab a tarp like this and dump it on the ground.

Fortunately, I didn't have to wait long.

"Just do exactly what I do," John Anderson said—as if I would have dared to do anything else.

He moved to the front right side of the car, motioned me to the rear right side of the car with a nod of his head, then reached down and began to pull the tarp straight up overhead. I did the same.

Yet, as much as I wanted to follow his lead, I couldn't help but be distracted by what came into view.

The car absolutely glistened.

First came the chrome bumper, then the light gray rear fender, then the bright burnished red of the taillight.

Each, in turn, glistened with a luster of its own.

Each part accentuated the other, magnified the other, transformed the other, enriched the other. It was love at first sight!

I can see that '47 Ford coupe as clearly and as wonderfully today as I saw it that first time in John Anderson's garage. As we lifted the tan tarp up and over the roof, folding it as he indicated—like a flag—with loving, deliberate attention, we slowly revealed each part of the car: first the chrome bumper, then the gray fender, the red taillight, the rear window, the roof, the trunk, the chrome trunk handle, until, all at once, they merged into a whole car, a presence—a shining gift—better than I would have dared to imagine, better than I possibly could have conceived in my mind's eye.

After completing the folding, John Anderson took the tarp, opened the trunk of the car, laid the folded tarp down inside, softly but firmly closed the trunk door, then stepped quietly aside, where he stood waiting without saying a word.

I think I said, "Wow!" but I can't be sure. If I did, it was to myself. The car held me in thrall.

The white walls, the chrome hubcaps, the deep, dark symmetrical tread of the tires, the windows, the chrome door handles, the fenders, the doors, the slow, lilting curve of the car itself—all came together into a luminescent statement about what a car could mean to a sixteen-year-old boy. More than anything I could have said, or John Anderson could have said, more than *anyone* could have said—this shimmering little Ford coupe, with its meticulous cleanliness, its deep sense of order, said it all.

Nothing could have been more to the point.

Nothing could have touched me any deeper.

Then John Anderson said, "Let's go for a ride."

There are four categories of preference that every business must satisfy in the minds and hearts of each of its four primary influencers.

■

Visual preferences, emotional preferences, functional preferences, and financial preferences make up what I call the E-Myth Enterprise Matrix.

John Anderson intuitively understood this idea.

* * *

To John Anderson, the sale of his 1947 Ford coupe was much more than a commercial transaction. Indeed, the car itself was much more than a car.

To John Anderson, his 1947 Ford coupe was an *idea*.

The sale of his 1947 Ford coupe was therefore an extension of that idea.

And so was John Anderson himself, and I, and, without knowing it, my parents and John Anderson's wife. All of us were an extension of that idea, all of us influencers, all of us influenced, all of us possessing preferences that needed to be satisfied—that *would be satisfied*—for the idea to become action, for the idea to move into its future and find itself joined with the world. Visual preferences, emotional preferences, functional preferences, financial preferences.

The idea of John Anderson's 1947 Ford coupe held within it all of the possibilities that would unfold—possibilities that were already there at the instant of its conception.

Within that particular 1947 Ford coupe resided the sixteen-year-old boy in both John Anderson and me, as well as all mothers, all fathers, all wives.

Each of us loved it, hated it, needed it, avoided it, wished it, dreamed it, created it, negated it, defended it, denied it, dreaded it—*lusted after it*—along with our relationships with each other; our relationships with ourselves; our ideas of a car; our ideas of buying, selling, and money; our ideas of every single unavoidable and interdependent part of this complex, subtle, and hopelessly entangled web of interactions and contradictions among the thoughts, feelings, and flesh of virtual strangers.

This, after all, was—and is—what the game called business is all about.

What was to become and has remained in my mind and heart—a successful business transaction for both John Anderson and me—never could have happened had not he instinctively, yet unwittingly, used the E-Myth Enterprise Matrix in his relationship with himself, my parents, his wife, and me.

As we drove, he talked.

"I guess you might say I have a passion for mechanical things: how they look; how they function; how they *exceed* their own limits; how they fit into the world. It's always been a passion of mine, for as long as I can remember."

He turned to look at me and said, "How about you? Does any of this mean anything to you?"

"I don't know," I answered.

But what John Anderson was saying reminded me of my saxophone teacher more than anything else.

"You and Merle would really get along," I suggested to him. "I've never known anybody as interested as Merle is in how to make things work as well as they possibly can. He's an absolute genius when it comes to fine-tuning my saxophone. All the while I figure my horn is about as good as it'll ever get, and then Merle does something to it, and it's a totally new horn! Is that what you mean?"

John Anderson was grinning from ear to ear.

"That's it exactly," he said. "That's what this car means to me. It's the perfect 1947 Ford coupe. If I wanted to buy a used car, I'd want it to look just fine like this. I'd want it to drive just like this. I'd want someone to have cared for it just like this—like it was the most important thing in the world. *Like whatever it could be, it was.*"

He turned down a quiet, tree-lined street, pulled up to the curb, and parked.

"Why don't you try it?" he said.

As I think back to it, it is as though I were fated to own that car.

As though the ad in the *Anaheim Bulletin* had been a letter written directly to me.

As though the 1947 Ford coupe in John Anderson's garage was waiting just for me.

As though he knew that I would be the only one to call, the only one to show up at his door, and that I would be the only one to drive away in his car. And that whatever needed to be done to accomplish that end, he would do, would handle, and would take responsibility for.

After driving the car back to his garage, replacing the tarp, and locking the garage door, we sat down at his kitchen table to talk business.

He never even asked me if I wanted to buy the car; it was a foregone conclusion.

Instead, we talked about my problems.

My parents, my money, and my need.

As we talked, a picture of the car waiting outside in the garage hovered in my mind.

As we talked, the feeling of the car's steering wheel lingered in my hands.

As we talked, I could feel the exhilarating sensation of driving quietly down the tree-lined street—in *my* car. I could see the fleeting, shimmering shadows of the leaves as they passed silently overhead—in *my* car. I could see the crystal-clear gleam of the windshield, the soft gray sheen of the sheets, and the deep burnished chrome dashboard John Anderson had had specially made—for *my* car.

As we talked, it was all over but the shouting.

John Anderson called my parents.

"It seems we have a problem," he said.

"Your son wants to buy my car, and I don't think we have a choice in the matter. But before we talk about it, I'd like for us to meet."

I could imagine my mother's dark, worried frown at the other end of the phone, my father's usual uncontrollable anger at being trapped into the discussion he didn't want to have—didn't need at this time. I waited for the explosion. But, surprisingly, it didn't come. John Anderson listened quietly and attentively for a moment or two, nodded affirmatively a few times, agreed to something apparently suggested by my parents, then hung up the phone.

They were coming over in thirty minutes, and I was to wait for them.

Need I paint you a picture of my parents coming to John Anderson's door, of how weird I felt standing in the home of someone who, only two hours before, had been a stranger (but who now, in some odd and unfathomable way, had taken on the mantle of a surrogate father for the special ritual that was unfolding before us)? Need I describe waiting for my parents to say hello, to acknowledge my presence, waiting for the thunder of their terrible anger at being caught up in this drama?

Need I paint you a picture of John Anderson's warm and respectful greeting—of the calm, gracious man my parents saw before them in his neat khaki clothes, in his neat and normal home, with his bright yet very calm blue eyes?

Need I describe his wife, who by now had become a very real participant in this strangely natural unfolding event, smiling warmly in her living room, inviting my parents to take a seat, the coffee and cookies they shared together, with me hovering on the fringes of their conversation like some nervous, fretting, anxious, and pestering old bird?

Need I paint a picture for you of the eventual walk to the garage—that mysterious, wondrous place that I had first walked to only two hours before? Out of respect for John Anderson and out of tolerance for me, my parents were going to look at this car, this troublesome thing that had suddenly brought so much unneeded emotion and disorder to their lives.

Need we take in the surprise I witnessed on their faces (especially my father's), as they saw what I had seen waiting in the garage, and as my father awkwardly performed the ritual with John Anderson and the spotless tan tarp that I had performed so awkwardly only a short time before?

I had never seen the boy in my father's face until that moment, and I never saw it again after that day.

Need I take you on the unnecessary but inevitable ride

the four of us took—like a hastily assembled family, my father too big and solid at the wheel for such an ephemeral occasion, John Anderson relaxed and smiling in the passenger's seat beside him, my mother and I sitting stiffly upright side by side in the small backseat like two dark birds on a telephone wire, staring straight ahead, afraid to look at each other for fear some spell might be broken and we would all suddenly and terribly disappear from the face of the earth? Such a strange and dreamy spectacle we must have seemed to people as we passed by on the road, as we carried out the many separate yet hyphenated steps of this extraordinary ritual.

Need we go through each of those still, quiet, intense, vivid, and unforgettable moments that led us all remarkably and uncomplainingly to the very end— that invisible, magical, and seamless point at which the pieces of this extraordinary yet ordinary ritual finally joined together as naturally and as effortlessly as two Velcro strips?

Need I say it? The deal was done!

VISUAL PREFERENCES, EMOTIONAL PREFERENCES, FUNCTIONAL PREFERENCES, AND FINANCIAL PREFERENCES

The potency and vitality of a business can only be actualized to the degree that it fills the possibilities to be discovered within each of these categories of preference as they are experienced by each of their four primary influencers.

If you do not believe me, see the car!

See the garage!

See John Anderson!

Feel the order, the control, the exquisite naturalness of this potentially disastrous event.

Everyone's preferences were served: my parents', John Anderson's, his wife's, and mine.

We all got exactly what we needed—what we wanted.

It was a marvel of synchronicity.

Let's take a look at the categories of preference one at a time.

* * *

DESIGNING THE ENTERPRISE: THE TAKEAWAY POINTS

(Listen to the Podcast version at MichaelEGerber.com)

■

There are four categories of preference that every business must satisfy in the minds and hearts of each of its four primary influencers.

- **Visual preferences**
- **Emotional preferences**
- **Functional preferences**
- **Financial preferences**

They make up what I call the E-Myth Enterprise Matrix. Each of these categories is accompanied by specific criteria that must be met if the enterprise is to be an E-Myth Enterprise.

Follow me on a journey that will make this clear and significant to you.

* * *

CHAPTER FOUR

THE FIRST CATEGORY OF PREFERENCE: THE VISUAL IDEAL

■

You never get a second chance to make a first impression.

—Anonymous

When I first read "The Red Wheelbarrow," a poem by William Carlos Williams, it was as a much younger man. But it wasn't until I found myself driving along a winding Sonoma County country road with a close friend on a rainy spring afternoon several years later that I fully appreciated it.

If you've never been there, the springtime hills in Sonoma County, California, are like a rolling green sea. Nestled between the waves are small ranches, oak and eucalyptus trees, low-lying brush, and outcroppings of brown jagged rock.

We were driving along a narrow fence-lined road when we came to a sharp turn. Upon turning the corner, we suddenly came face-to-face with a scene so vivid, so striking, that I can clearly remember every part of it to this day.

It was a small, yellow ranch house, with bright green trim around the eaves and white molding around the windows and the door.

As we turned the corner, the sun came out from behind a storm cloud and struck the house, transforming it into a blaze of yellow light shot up from the ground and blinding me with its radiance. My friend must also have been temporarily blinded, because he slammed on the breaks, and we skidded to a halt directly in front of the small house's fenced front yard.

Standing before us in the middle of the yard, halfway between the fence and the house, was a large, glowing, bright red, meticulously cared for antique wagon. The drops of rainwater streaming down its sides glistened in the sun like diamonds.

But that wasn't all, for surrounding the wagon was a yard full of pure white turkeys, their red wattles bobbing up and down.

Can you see it?

Can you feel it?

Can you hold this image in your mind? Do you

wonder whose yard it is, and why the wagon, and had someone just fed the turkeys? What smells do you associate with this picture? What feelings come to mind? What thoughts arise from your past, from your imagination, from ideas you had about such things when you were a young boy or girl, or even now, as you are today?

Can you see how profoundly we're touched by such visual images?

It should become immediately obvious to you how important the conception, creation, and maintenance of a strong visual impression is to the ultimate success of a business.

A business, like a farmyard—like an old country road—is first and foremost a visual thing. What a business looks like communicates more about its thoughts, feelings, considerations, and intentions, more immediately and more lastingly—more *humanly*—to the people with whom it interacts than anything else that business can do.

As William Carlos Williams said, "*So much depends upon it!*"

And so much does.

It is virtually impossible for anyone to see anything without drawing an instantaneous, if unconscious, conclusion about it.

In fact, it is not so much that we quickly draw conclusions about what we see, but that the conclusions we draw were already drawn long before we saw it.

Each of us possesses (or, more accurately, is possessed by) a vast underground visual storehouse we call our *unconscious*.

This storehouse, our unconscious—this picture book—is bursting with a rich, complex assortment of visual symbols, associations, interpretations, judgments, meanings, feelings, and physical reactions—in short, conclusions—all of which conspire automatically with each other with laserlike speed, to shape our very existence.

What we wear, what we drive, where we work, where and how we live, what we think—the very objects, spaces, colors, distances, forms, and people we surround ourselves with, and by which we're surrounded—are all significant parts of this extraordinarily complex web of visual conclusions each of us has formed.

A mother nursing her child; a grandmother preparing the Thanksgiving turkey for her grown-up children and her grandchildren; a young father roughhousing with his son and their Labrador retriever in the backyard; that same man, grown gray, showing his grandson how to tune a carburetor in a period truck; a tall, distinguished man in an impeccably tailored dark navy blue suit, waiting outside a contemporary office building—all are pictures, visual representations of deeply held conclusions we all have made some time in our lives. They may even be representative of Carl Jung's archetypes—pictures we all share, pictures that touch us all in much the same way.

There are an infinite number of such pictures, waiting to be understood, waiting to be identified, but working unconsciously in each and every one of us in the same way. No matter what any of us thinks, they shape our lives.

Do you see what I mean? Do you understand the importance of this concept?

So much depends upon it!

If all that we see touches us so immediately, so completely; if every visual impression we receive causes each of us to feel, think, and act in a certain preprogrammed— if not totally predictable—way (and it does!), is it any wonder, then, that the conception, creation, and maintenance of the visual impression of a business is so critical to its success?

Should it come as such a surprise to you when I say that to conceive, create, and successfully maintain an extraordinarily effective business—an E-Myth Enterprise—has much more to do with the management of *impressions* than it has to do with the management of people?

The management of impressions *is* the management of people.

And visual impressions are the most powerful impressions of all.

The problem seems to be that the vast majority of businesses in this country—small or large—simply don't get it, or what's worse, simply don't care.

The "search for excellence" in theory seems somehow to have eluded us in practice.

Contrary to popular belief, there's an overwhelming poverty of the entrepreneurial spirit in this country.

Walk or drive down just about any commercial street or walk inside just about any business you choose, and you'll immediately be accosted by the visual symptoms of our entrepreneurial malaise.

Signs, windows, sidewalks, buildings, trucks, employees' dress, bathrooms, floors, countertops, aisles, walls—rundown, dirty, worn out, unimaginative, decaying, cluttered, confusing—a visual mess!—businesses disintegrating right before our eyes.

Yet all those signs were new once, all the windows newly installed; all the floors, the walls, the bathrooms, the desks, the file cabinets, the trucks, the automobiles, the forklifts, the merchandise racks, every single element of every business was at the outset a function of someone's dream. What happened? What stopped working? What do people think as they go to work there, as they buy there? *What are the owners thinking?*

I believe it could be proven that a visually deteriorating business is the act of an emotionally deteriorating mind.

What do people feel as they are visually accosted every day of their lives by all of this negativity, neglect, and disinterest?

Well, let me tell you a story.

There once was a relatively small company that was struggling against great odds to gain market share from a huge Goliath of a company. The little company sputtered for years, suffering from poor leadership and a mix of nearly indistinguishable products that confused consumers, that performed poorly, that were unattractive in design. Their already meager market share continued to plummet, as did the value of their stock. They were on the verge of going away forever when someone had a brilliant idea: "Let's bring back one of our original founders to run the place. He appears to be the last person associated with this company who had any sort of vision."

So they did. They brought in a founding partner to be the new CEO. So dire was the financial condition of the company—but so much faith did the new CEO have in its potential—that he agreed to return to work for an annual salary of one dollar, plus stock options.

He began to turn things around almost immediately. He oversaw the design of a sleek new product and soon thereafter offered it in a range of bright colors that were mimicked by scores of other companies that manufactured everything from ring binders to kitchen blenders. The product took off. It set a new standard for visual preference in terms of color.

Success followed success, until one day in 2001, the CEO stood in front of a crowd at the company's annual convention and announced a new product that would revolutionize an entire industry, and eventually account for 70 percent of a particular market.

Yes, that CEO is Steve Jobs. The company, of course,

is Apple. The long list of revolutionary products includes the original colorful iMac, the iPod, iTunes, and the iPhone. The company is no longer on the verge of extinction, and the stock options (along with his Pixar Animation Studios investment, of course) proved to be a good thing for Steve Jobs. He is now, among other things, the Walt Disney Company's largest single shareholder.

Through its products, its packaging, and its retail stores, Apple demonstrates how important the visual ideal is to business.

Let me tell you another story that will further illuminate this point for you. It's about two brothers who owned a great store.

Not that it was always a great store—it wasn't.

Indeed, if you had seen it when I first saw it, you'd have had to agree with me that, in Marty and Sol Weissberg's business, a visual renaissance has since taken place.

"A transformation," Marty called it.

"A miracle," said Sol.

But whatever you'd call it, it happened this way.

* * *

Several years ago, Marty Weissberg was called home from graduate school at the University of San Francisco to help his older brother, Sol, run the family business after their father, Morris, died unexpectedly at the young age of fifty-three.

Fortunately for both of them, the business, Weiss-berg's Army-Navy Surplus Store, sort of ran itself, if only in a lackluster way.

Customers came and went; employees too. Nobody seemed to know why.

Although Sol and Marty had both served their apprenticeship in the business from the ages of eight and ten, respectively, most of their time had been spent at their father's beck and call, unpacking the green, gray, blue, brown, and black military merchandise that arrived in enormous brown cardboard boxes from who-knew-where and pricing it according to their father's cryptic, hand-printed instructions, using a pricing strategy only Morris understood. They then stacked the merchandise on the already jam-packed shelves or hung it on the special racks that their father ordered them to move around the store at what were apparently strategically significant times of the week or the month—from the back of the store to the front, to either the right side or the left, down the middle aisle or by the cash register. On clear, sunny days, some merchandise was moved to the sidewalk and ceremoniously labeled SALE in bright red letters (even though both Marty and Sol knew that the prices hadn't been changed).

Marty and Sol swept the floors, threw out the trash, cleaned the windows, and occasionally—only occasionally—were entrusted to "work with the customers" who their father seemed to *know* wouldn't buy, and rarely did.

Morris dealt with all the rest—the "real" customers.

Unfortunately—and despite the long, dreary, chore-filled hours they spent in the store after school and on weekends for most of their adolescent years—neither Marty nor Sol "knew the business," as their father was given to say. Morris was so busy working the store that he had never gotten around to teaching them.

And then he died, and the store was theirs—a business both Marty and Sol hated, not only for all the time it had taken from them as boys, but for their inability—now that they could finally be free of it once and for all—to say good-bye to it, to let go of it, and finally to get on with the purpose of their individual lives.

Perhaps that was it. There was no purpose.

To Marty and Sol, if there was a life other than the business, they didn't know what it was. So they lived the only one they knew.

For the first six months or so, Sol and Marty glowered at each other across distances of their own making, repeating in silence the dreary rituals of their boyhoods past.

But now, without their father to goad them on, the rituals were even more lifeless than before.

No Morris was there to tell them to move the racks.

No Morris was there to remind them to paint the red SALE signs.

No Morris exhorted them to sweep the floors, to
take out the trash, or to wash the windows.

No, there was no Morris there to do it, so Sol did it.

He did the only thing he could think to do: he
became Morris. He became the father the two of them
had lost.

One day he was Sol, the next day, Morris. Sol, in fact,
became the chief proponent of "OldCo." He was doing
the things of the past, in the ways of the past.

He began to spend long hours after the store was
closed, while Marty had gone home to rummage through
his father's effects, to seek out clues—a trail, a sign, that
could teach him what his father never did—that could
teach him what his father knew.

A new light in Marty was beginning to form. Marty
was beginning to awaken to the exhilarating possibility
that he was now, finally, free to become himself. Marty
became an inspired Dreamer, eager to transform "OldCo"
into "NewCo."

You could see it in his eyes.

* * *

A friend of mine who worked closely with Walt Disney
for more than fifteen years related to me what it was that
made Disney a special man to all those who knew him.

"He had the innate ability to see things whole in a completely original way," my friend said.

"Where everyone else in a meeting would be caught up in specifics, Walt could *see* the finished product, he could envision what everyone else seemed to miss—the magic that lived within every project just beneath the surface, waiting to be discovered."

"That's where Walt lived," my friend told me, "in the magic beneath the surface of things. And only when he revealed what he saw there did it become obvious to everyone else *that it was there all the time.*"

That, I might suggest, is also where Marty Weissberg in his own small, but not insignificant, way was beginning to live—beneath the surface of things.

Indeed, I believe that it is there, *beneath* the surface of things, where the surface, the true reality, actually resides.

■

And so it is that the visual preference is so immediately critical to the success of a business.

* * *

One day that thought came to Marty. It hit him square between the eyes. Marty clearly saw, for the very first time, what had *always* been there, had haunted him throughout his childhood, had clung to him like an oppressive gray fog as he left school every day on his way to the store, had waited for him like that enormous, grotesque Sumatran toad he had once seen at the zoo, squatting motionless as a stone in its small glass aquarium, its mottled brown lumpy skin glistening in the green-gray tropical light. *It was all so ugly!*

From the front of the store, with its faded red neon letters spelling out the family name in belligerent block letters fourteen feet long and four feet high across the squat, square face of the old brick building, to the inside of the store, with its low, brown tin ceiling and its rows of fluorescent lights, which could never brighten the darkness of the store beneath them; from the black, perennially soiled linoleum floors, the gray metal racks with their squeaky rubber wheels, and the rows of dark metal shelves, to the hand-lettered signs hanging from the ceiling telling the customers where to find—among the bewildering array of sloppily stacked merchandise— the pants, jackets, boots, socks, belts, knives, canteens, shirts, hats, tents, sleeping bags, mosquito nets, socket wrenches, and all the other exotic military paraphernalia known as surplus—it all displayed a blatant lack of attention, of care, of imagination, of interest.

Then there was the back of the store: the massive, rusted, steel-framed doors; the thick, scarred, ancient planks of the floor and the loading dock, stained black from years of abuse; the swollen, cracked, and tortured asphalt of the narrow, twisting alley with its ever-present trash, broken bottles, overflowing garbage cans, and sagging chain-link fences running between the dark-stained brick back walls of the neighboring stores.

Finally, there was the bathroom: small and dank, like a cold, sweaty closet, with its unpainted concrete floor, both the wash bowl and toilet stained and streaked after years of use; with its solitary, naked hundred-watt bulb hanging from the impenetrable shadows above, the only other light coming from a small window above the sink, barred against forcible entry (as though anyone would want to break in there!). The whole room was filthy from years of neglect. The dirt, the cobwebs, and whatever other indescribable blight had risen from the alley behind the store had crusted over the window and cast a yellow, spotted pall over the peeling, damp brown door and walls.

As a boy, Marty would do anything other than go to the bathroom in that store, and when he finally couldn't wait any longer, he'd go down the street to the gas station at the corner, where at least the restroom was clean.

At last, Marty fully understood what it was about the store that so deeply depressed him.

Despite what Marty had always believed to be true about his father—that he loved nothing else but his business, that he cared for nothing else but the store—Marty now knew that exactly the opposite was true.

He knew that the store had so angered Morris—so infuriated him, so consumed him—that there was simply nothing left for anyone, or anything, else.

It wasn't the fact that *he* hated the store that depressed Marty so much, but that his *father* had.

The ugliness of Weissberg's Army-Navy was a mute but eloquent testament to the fact that his father felt himself—and then became—a prisoner there, until the only way out was to die.

So that was the madness that Marty saw in Sol's eyes.

Like his father before him, Sol too had become a prisoner of the store. Like his father before him, the store enraged Sol. Like his father before him, the store became Sol's justification for not living. First for Morris, and now for Sol, the store had become the ugly fact of their absence of love for what they were doing and of the life they had both given up to do it.

And, like Morris, Sol mistakenly thought that by possessing the store, by owning it—*by keeping it his secret*—he could ultimately get even.

Only Marty knew different.

* * *

At Disneyland, it takes 5,000 gallons of paint each year to keep the park looking better than new. There are 500,000 costume pieces to maintain and more than

100,000 lightbulbs that have to be changed as they burn out. Then there are the gardens, the restaurants, and the myriad other small, insignificant tasks associated with the visual preparation of Disneyland for every day the park opens for business, just as Walt had envisioned it in his dream of the business back at the beginning when most people thought him to be crazy ("You want to do *what*?"), when the park was just an outsized, elaborate, and insane idea, which, according to common business wisdom at the time (and at this time, and for all times, it seems), could never be justified economically. It was that idealistic.

McDonald's has more than 31,000 locations, and its nearly half million employees serve 47 million customers daily. Recent estimates reveal that it costs the company more than $7 million a day to perform the daily ritual of visually preparing the floors, the equipment, the windows, the parking lots, the sidewalks, the signage, the counters, the uniforms, and the equipment—all the unavoidable and integral parts of the visual integrity of the McDonald's corporate image as imagined by its founder, Ray Kroc, at the very outset of the business when he had crew people clean up all the litter within a block of each restaurant.

At Federal Express, it costs an estimated $70,000 a day to steam wash the company's 30,000 internationally recognized trucks to make certain that FedEx maintains its visual impact as it was envisioned by Fred Smith, long before the business began, long before the first truck rolled out the door.

* * *

Marty and I talked about the miraculous transformation of his and Sol's business.

"I swear," Marty said to me, "it struck me just like that."

He continued, a dark light growing in his eyes.

"There was the mourning period, of course, even though I didn't realize that's what I was doing at the time.

"Naturally, Sol and I mourned in different ways. To Sol, mourning was an act of honoring the past. He felt somehow that he had let our father down, that he had disappointed him, that if he had taken a more active interest in the business, our father wouldn't have died. So he was compelled to act out every little thing my father did, exactly as my father would have done it.

"To me," Marty continued, "mourning was an act of grieving for my lost childhood, the games I never played, the playing we never did as a family, the lack of pure joy in our life.

"At first I thought it was just Sol who was going crazy. But then I came to realize that we both were. But, of course, we had no childhood. Our father was a lunatic. He raised us to be lunatics. We were simply acting out his wishes.

"Gradually, deep in my heart, I began to feel a sharp, aching, almost unbearable pain for the extraordinary price my father had made Sol and me pay as children: the loss of joy, the loss of imagination, the loss of curiosity, of color, of vitality, of creativity, the loss of our childhood, the loss of ourselves.

"I swear I carried the pain of that loss around with me every day, from the day I came home to the store after my father died, to the day that the light turned itself on in my heart.

"And, suddenly, I found myself free, not as a twenty-four-year-old man, but as a boy. It suddenly became clear to me, not so much something I thought, but in a burst of feeling so strong, so deeply compelling, that I began to sob uncontrollably. I must have cried for hours.

"This might sound stupid to you," Marty said to me, almost apologetically, as though what he was about to say would be impossible for me to understand, "but it was like I fell in love with myself as a boy. It was like I had, in an instant, become both the father I wish I'd had and the boy I wish I could have been. And it was like the father I had now become touched me, his son, and said, 'Trust your heart! Whatever you need to do, do it! Don't wait! There's time enough to die. I love you.'"

Marty continued, almost in a whisper, tears welling in his eyes, "At that moment, I loved my father more than I could ever remember. I could finally cry for him, for the loss of *his* childhood, for the terrible price he had paid for being a prisoner in a prison of his own making. God, how desperate he must have been."

He was quiet for a moment, then went on.

"And what happened, when I was reunited with myself, with this strange but wonderful little boy I had been, I finally realized that I was suddenly free to do anything I wished with the store. I could sell it. I could give it away. I could give my share to Sol. I could even *burn it down* if I wanted. Our father was gone. The prison door was open. There was no track to follow but my own. I didn't need permission anymore!"

* * *

The visual transformation of a business is an emotional thing; it comes best from the heart. It is a creation that when done exceedingly well is always endowed with a pure passion to touch something beyond the ordinary— the most human of expressions, a statement of dignity, of caring, of consideration, but most of all, of love.

It has less to do with the business as a commercial enterprise than it has to do with the business as a *human* enterprise—its relationship with people, their ideas, and the things that connect people and their ideas with the world around them.

In this regard, the business doesn't only produce products, it becomes the product of the people by whom and for whom it is created.

To effectively differentiate the business-as-a-product from all other businesses, a business must be a visual interpretation of a specific and well thought out point of view or philosophy regarding the questions we humans have asked of ourselves since time immemorial—questions of freedom, of God, of law, of integrity, of purpose, of loyalty, of service, of honor, of order, of beauty, of self-respect and respect for others, and many more.

In short, to rise above the ordinary, a business must become a visual statement of belief, of meaning—a medium through which people communicate with one another about what they believe in, what they care for, what is important to them.

Taken to that level, the visualization of a business is an art form. And just like a work of art, there are at least six tangible components that comprise the Visual Matrix that need to be considered in the construction of a business.

■

These six components are color, form, scale, order, detail, and information.

Color. Color is the first thing people see and is therefore a critical component of the Visual Matrix. What colors will best communicate the purpose of the business? Is the business playful? Is it serious? Is it upbeat? Is it formal? Is the business intended to touch the hearts of people, just their minds, or both their hearts and minds?

When I say "playful," do certain colors come to mind? When I say "somber," do you see the dark colors it evokes? When I say "upbeat," can you visualize what those colors might be? Can you hear the *sounds* such colors make?

Form. What form does the business take—from the logo, to the style of dress, to the architecture, to the products? Is it bold, adventurous, sedate, austere, comfortable, or powerful? Does it call for rounded, soft edges or sharp, angular edges? Or are there few edges at all?

Can you imagine in your mind's eye what form a comfortable business might take? Do you remember the old yellow ranch house, with its small flock of white turkeys and its antique red wagon? Was that comfortable, or was it adventurous? Can you imagine Thanksgiving in such a place? The family around the table; Grandma in her wire-rimmed glasses; Granddad grinning at his youngest grandson, who is sitting in his highchair and throwing food across the table; everyone chattering, about the past, the present, the future; food streaming and plentiful on the huge dining room table? Comfortable? Austere? Sedate? Powerful? When you know what you wish to communicate in your business, the form will almost immediately appear.

Scale. And what of the scale of the business? Is it built for people, or is it built to intimidate people? Does it take our breath away, or does it make us laugh? Does it say, "This is going to be one hell of a good time," as Disneyland says, stretching out as it does as far as the eye can see, or does it confine us so that we simply want to get out? Is it the scale of a Gothic church or of a miniature railroad? A Gothic church is not built for comfort; a miniature railroad does not convey power.

Order. Order is such a critical component of the visual business that I am continually amazed at how oblivious most businesses seem to be to the price they pay every single day for ignoring it. Order is just what it says: it is all things in their place; it is cleanliness; it is impeccability; it is a deep, abiding sense of control—that there is a logic, a sensitivity, a commitment to keeping the jungle out of the clearing; it is a belief in the special quality of human life; it is the meticulous attention paid to the maintenance—to the surface of things, of sustaining the newness, the freshness, the essence of things as we have envisioned them new. Order is preparing the ground before us as though God himself were to visit.

Detail. Once people have walked in the door, once they have taken a closer look, it is the attention to detail that they begin to notice: the shining copper rivets, exactly placed two inches apart on the aluminum wastebaskets; the specially designed pin with the company's logo on the shirts or aprons of every employee. Detail is the care one puts into all the little things of the business, so as people look closer, they are surprised by what they find.

Information. Every business must find a visual way to transmit information to its customers, its employees, its suppliers, and its lenders—the information they each perceive they need—in the most visually compelling way possible. A small business consulting firm covers its reception area walls with "Impact Reports"—letters from its clients—telling the world how their business is improving. A pet store places charmingly informative picture cards next to each cage, describing the inhabitant's traits as a pet, as well as where they came from, what they eat, whether they are good for children, and the amount of care they require. An auto body shop provides its customers with a large glass window looking onto the shop floor, where its employees go about their specialized tasks in uniforms and with equipment color-coded by function, while a CD playing over a PA system describes what the customer is watching.

Of course, there are options in all of this.

Whether it be a meat market, a grocery store, an auto dealership, a semiconductor plant, a church, or an Apple Computer store, the visualization of a business can be either reduced to the merely pragmatic or raised to the ideal. It can be ordinary or sublime.

But it is certain that the higher one reaches, the more power one feels.

* * *

Given their different perspectives, it wasn't easy for either of them, but Marty and Sol began to talk.

At first, Sol reminded Marty of Morris. He got angry, he stormed away from his office. He'd stay hunkered down at his desk for days.

But gradually, over a period of several months, as Marty described it, "Morris finally let go of him."

"The truth was," Marty went on, "that Sol and I had more in common with each other than we ever did with our father."

They began to talk.

They began to share.

They began to feel what it was like to be brothers.

At long last the gulf between them vanished, and Marty told Sol what he had in mind.

"I want this place to become a place of light," Marty said.

"I want people to come from all over town just to see it, whether they buy something or not.

"I want to put in a small restaurant, a coffee shop, and an indoor playground for little kids to play in while their parents walk around the store, with someone to watch them and take care of them for as long as their parents want.

"I want there to be a small stream running through the playground, with a waterfall roaring down from the ceiling. And I want koi fish—golden and white and black spotted koi swimming in the stream, with green plants, and a place for the kids to feed the fish three times a day, and a small petting zoo, with lambs, and pygmy goats, and miniature horses. I want the place to be bright, and open, and colorful, and most of all I want it to be clean, spotless, absolutely perfect.

"I want it to be fun, too. I want people to love being here—our employees, and our customers, and you, Sol, and me. I want to tear out the ceiling and go straight up to the roof joists to give us some room to breathe! I want to tear out the wallboard and sandblast the brick walls until they're absolutely new, bright red and white. I want to tear up the linoleum and lay down thin strips of clear white oak, intermixed with brick and flagstone paths leading to the garden at the base of the waterfall.

"I want to have bright grass-green antique benches located throughout the store, so that if people want to take a load off their feet, they can.

"I want there to be music, not Muzak, but real music, a live piano, or a string quartet, and sometimes, just for the hell of it, a small rock band, to give the place a kick in the ass!

"I want to market *colorful* products; no more dark blue, black, green, gray, and brown, but bright blue, and red, and yellow, and green, and products for camping, hiking, fishing, hunting, all outdoor recreation and sports. And I want them to be displayed colorfully, dramatically, with big colorful plastic keys given to the customers when they walk in the door to use in video terminals to provide them with all the information they'll need about the more difficult-to-understand products, so that they'll never have to ask anyone where anything is, or what it does, or what the difference is between one product or another.

"Can you see it, Sol?

"And that's only the beginning. I want this place to shine! And I want something grand, something absolutely astonishing, something totally unexpected and stunning suspended from the ceiling by invisible wire to swoop down on the customers as they walk in the front door. Perhaps one month it will be a giant glider, or another month a real biplane, or—even better—how about an incredible true-to-life model of an American bald eagle with eighteen-foot wings stretched out on either side, staring down at everyone with its huge, sharp yellow, eagle eyes!

"Most of all, Sol, I want to change our name and the face of the building, and I want the sign to soar up from the roof so that no one can possibly miss it. And I want the sign to say

FLYING HIGH & FIELDSTONE GREEN!"

Marty reached behind him, took out a large brown paper–wrapped package, tore it open, and turned the art board within it around so that Sol could see.

Sol stared at the illustration and blinked twice before saying, "But, what does it *mean*?"

Marty began to laugh, then to roar, holding his sides, tears welling from his eyes.

"It means, old buddy, things are about to change."

* * *

That store succeeded. In fact, it exceeded all of Marty's expectations. Sol watched all of this in amazement. Weissberg's Army-Navy Surplus became a sporting goods/camping/mountain-climbing empire, with stores everywhere.

Can you guess what that chain, that empire, is called today? No, it's not Weissberg's. It's not even

FLYING HIGH & FIELDSTONE GREEN!

Can you guess? You'd probably be wrong.

But I can tell you this: the six components of the

Visual Matrix all come together in perfect unison at this amazing enterprise.

On your next (or first) visit to a Starbucks, an Apple store, a FedEx office, or a similar business, challenge yourself to notice the interplay of the six components of the Visual Matrix: color, form, scale, order, detail, and information.

* * *

DESIGNING THE ENTERPRISE:
THE TAKEAWAY POINTS

**(Listen to the Podcast version
at MichaelEGerber.com)**

■

The visual ideal is vital to every business in every industry. The conception, creation, and maintenance of the visual impression of a business is critical to its success.

The problem seems to be that the vast majority of businesses in this country—small or large—simply don't get it, or what's worse, simply don't care. Walk or drive down just about any commercial street or walk inside just about any business you choose, and you'll immediately be accosted by the visual symptoms of our entrepreneurial malaise. I believe it could be proven that a visually deteriorating business is the act of an emotionally deteriorating mind, of leadership on the verge of failure.

The six components of visual preference are color, form, scale, order, detail, and information.

Color is the first thing people see and is therefore a critical component of the Visual Matrix.

Form follows color in the order of importance. What form does the business take—from the logo, to the style of dress, to the architecture, to the products?

Scale is next. Is the business built for people, or is it built to intimidate people? Does it take our breath away, or does it make us laugh? Does it say (as Disneyland announces the moment you walk through the gates), "This is going to be one hell of a good time!"

Fourth in the Visual Matrix is *order*. Order is just what it says: it is all things in their place; it is cleanliness; it is impeccability; it is a deep, abiding sense of control; it is the meticulous attention paid to the maintenance— to the surface of things, of sustaining the newness, the freshness, the essence of things as we have envisioned them new.

Fifth in importance is *detail*. Detail is the care one puts into all the little things of the business, so as people look closer, they are surprised by what they find.

And sixth, is *information*. Every business must find a visual way to transmit meaningful information to its customers, its employees, its suppliers, and its lenders— the information they each perceive they need—in the most visually compelling way possible.

For a successful enterprise, "serving up" the visual ideal is not an option. It's a necessity.

* * *

CHAPTER FIVE

THE SECOND CATEGORY OF PREFERENCE: THE EMOTIONAL IDEAL

Man is a rope stretched between the animal and the Superman—a rope over an abyss. A dangerous crossing, a dangerous wayfaring, a dangerous looking-back, a dangerous trembling and halting.

—Friedrich Nietzsche, *Thus Spake Zarathustra*

To become an E-Myth Enterprise, it is essential for a business to become a visual production. But for the production to have meaning, for the form to have substance, the second category of preference, the emotional ideal, is equally essential, lest the production degenerate into what might be called visual rhetoric, "full of sound and fury, signifying nothing."

Is business a form of war? Consider the long conflict in Iraq.

Fighting in the desert, surrounded by nothingness, a man or woman runs the risk of losing sight of why he or she is there, except to survive. A soldier's motivation becomes doubly important. I believe that U.S. officers involved in any conflict should make the effort to take the time to sit with their troops, to explain goals, to know every soldier personally, to give them the feeling that they are the best and that their mission is vital.

Leadership is at a premium in any war, and without it, nothing will be achieved.

It might be argued that the comparison between war and business is an unreasonable one; that war brings with it a special edge, a unifying principle, that is impossible to sustain in an ordinary business engaged in mundane commercial transactions where life and death is not a day-to-day question, if a question at all.

I believe the opposite is true.

I believe a great business becomes so to the degree that, like war, it raises serious questions. It brings us face-to-face with our own mortality. If there are no extrahuman challenges, it creates them and engages with its own resistance to change the desert of its own doubt. It forms its people into squads, and companies, and regiments, and battalions, and divisions and determines where the enemy is (it is always within), and launches, time and time again, into battle after battle, if only to take one yard at a time, to experience not so much the land that is acquired (although, of course, there is that), but the extraordinary inner strength that is developed, the camaraderie, the passion that is shared, passed on, handed from person to person, from heart to heart; a sense of purpose, of value, of being as fully human as we can be, given our limited understanding, our limited skill, our limited interest.

In his book *The Master Game*, Robert S. de Ropp says:

What people really need and demand from life is not wealth, comfort or esteem, but *games worth playing.* He who cannot find a game worth playing is apt to fall prey to *accidie,* defined by the Fathers of the Church as one of the Deadly Sins, but now regarded as a symptom of sickness. Accidie is a paralysis of the will, a failure of the appetite, a condition of generalized boredom, total disenchantment—"God, oh God, how weary, stale, flat and unprofitable seem to me all the uses of this world!" Such a state of mind . . . is a prelude to what is loosely called "mental illness," which . . . fills half the beds in hospitals and makes multitudes of people a burden to themselves, their families, and to society. . . . Seek, above all, for a game worth playing. Such is the advice of the oracle to modern man. Having found the game, play it with intensity—play as if your life and sanity depended on it. (They *do* depend on it.) Follow the example of the

French existentialists and flourish a banner bearing the word "engagement."

Though nothing means anything and all roads are marked "NO EXIT," yet move as if your movements had some purpose. If life does not seem to offer a game worth playing, then *invent one*. For it must be clear, even to the most clouded intelligence, that any game is better than no game.*

"What is a game?" de Ropp asks. "It is essentially a trial of strength by rules. Rules are essential. If the rules were not observed, the game would cease to be a game at all. A meaningful game of chess would be impossible if one player insisted on treating all pawns as queens."

De Ropp goes on to say that the only game worth playing is what he calls "the Master Game," the aim of which is "true awakening, full development of the powers latent in man."

Most of the people I know are not confused enough.

Oh, they would all admit to a certain degree of frustration, doubt, a lack of certainty as to how a particularly vexing problem could best be solved.

Like how to get Jack to show up for work on time.

Or how to get the landlord to fix the air conditioner, which, no matter what we say or do, blasts on at the coldest time of the day and shuts off at the warmest.*

---

* *The Master Game: Beyond the Drug Experience,* de Roop, Robert S. New York: Dell, 1974.

But, aside from these petty frustrations that manage to bollix up our day from time to time, to my way of thinking none of that is what I would call a true confusion.

A true confusion means total disorientation.

Most people I know live moment to moment, state to state, voicing their opinions on just about everything, and, in the process, confirming their existence—the certainty of themselves. We all do it. It's a matter of habit. How else would we get on with life?

But what I'm saying is that most of the people I know are not confused enough.

They rarely stop to see how little they actually *do* know—about anything.

They rarely, if ever, put themselves into question.

They rarely, if ever, get to the point where they suddenly feel totally stupid.

Indeed, they rarely, if ever, allow themselves to feel stupid, because it's not only scary to feel that way, to see how absolutely stupid we are all concerning just about everything, but it's drop-dead terrifying to come face-to-face with the dark, deep abyss of how little we actually know, and, even worse, with the alarming, unsettling, absolutely devastating fact that most of the time *we're not even here.*

If we were to be honest with each other, we would have to agree that most people are like that. In fact, if we really want to be honest with each other, if the truth were really to be revealed—*you and I are like that.*

Oh, yes we are. We're all certifiable dummies.

What's worse, we're all mainly gone, absent, asleep, out to lunch most of the time, habit-ridden, doing an automatic dance of someone else's choosing, pushed along from behind.

It's my contention that if we were working in a great business, *someone would be telling us that all the time.*

Someone would be reminding us that we're not confused enough, that we have too many stupid answers and not enough questions occupying our minds.

A great business makes sure to keep *everyone* awake—its customers, its employees, its suppliers, and its lenders.

True, it's a difficult, often treacherous, path to take.

Most people don't like to be confused. They don't like to be jostled; they don't like to feel jarred; they don't like to have someone say, "Think!" as Tom Watson at IBM was given to do; and they like to have opinions about everything that goes on. Don't we? Don't we all like that, honest to God, deep down inside, don't we all like to be *authorities*?

On the other hand, isn't there a part of us, however small and timid, that loves to be shaken?

For it's that shock to awaken, it's that cosmic rap on the noggin, it's that existential kick in the ass, it's that primordial shout from our struggling old conscience that says, "Wake up! Wake up! Wake up!" that lifts us out of the ether, that snaps us out of our lockstep, that pins us to the wall of our sleep and makes us look at it, makes us open our eyes, makes us breathe, think, move, *come alive*!

I had a saxophone teacher once. As I mentioned earlier, his name was Merle.

Merle was a tyrant, a tormentor. Other than the fact that he was a genius at the saxophone, he had nothing else going for him.

Merle must have weighed at least 300 pounds. He had a drinking problem, too. Not that I ever saw him drunk, though I don't think I would have known it if he had been. I was only nine years old when I started studying with him. But at each one of my hour-long Saturday morning lessons (there were at least 400 of them in all: I studied with him for almost eight years), he drank down a whole quart of beer. Now, I know he had other students besides me, about seven every day. That means that Merle drank at least seven quarts of beer a day for the entire time I knew him, and not once did I see him out of control.

(The only symptom Merle ever displayed to me of his possible alcohol problem was a broken leg he suffered shortly after I began studying with him. He wore a cast, which stayed with him, off and on, for the rest of his life. He told me that he'd been jumped by two drunks in a bar one night; one of them held him, while the second propped up his leg between two chairs, and then beat it with a bat. Needless to say the leg never healed, and it finally killed him—the leg, not the alcohol—but I don't really think it matters which to Merle.)

Merle and I had an understanding.

This was the deal: Merle could beat the living hell out of me (not literally, but figuratively), and I was free to quit if I didn't like it.

And he exercised his part of the bargain almost every week.

He was the most difficult man I have ever known in my life.

He wouldn't allow me to get away with anything.

If I let up a little on my practicing, he knew it.

If I played something sloppily, or carelessly, or thoughtlessly, he called me on it, every single time, and made me play it over and over and over again, until I got it just right.

Understand, to Merle, "just right" meant perfect, absolutely right.

And it didn't matter to Merle if the entire hour was taken up with one simple phrase. That's what we'd do, that one phrase, over and over and over again, until it fairly flew from my fingers on its own.

To get to Merle's, I'd take a bus from Anaheim to downtown Los Angeles, then transfer to a second bus that would take me to North Hollywood, where Merle's studio was. It was a long trip, up and back: at least three hours of bus riding for every hour of saxophone lesson.

But it didn't matter to Merle how many buses I took, or how far I had to come to study with him, or how young I was, or, for that matter, how big a pain in the ass he could be as a teacher.

Nothing mattered to Merle but the bargain we had struck: that it was his lot in life to teach people to become great saxophone players, and that people studied with him for exactly that reason.

And to Merle, anything I did, or failed to do, that violated that bargain was grounds for immediate, and drastic, action.

On one occasion, only two minutes into the lesson, Merle coolly told me to pack up my saxophone and go back home. The lesson was over. When I asked him why, he looked at me in disgust, and said, "Go."

I never did find out why he asked me to go home that particular day, but deep down in my heart I knew the reason.

It was because Merle knew I wasn't working as hard as I could.

Merle knew that I had a lazy streak in me a mile wide.

And I knew it, too!

He wasn't only telling me to go home early, he was telling me to look at myself, to put myself into question, to ask myself whether or not I was really serious about becoming a great saxophone player. Was I taking myself as seriously as Merle was?

Was I keeping my part of the bargain?

I honestly can't tell you what kept me going back to get beat up by Merle week after week, month after month, year after year. But I think it was the sound of my saxophone, as it changed, and grew, and matured—as it became music. Its depth, its range, its richness, its dexterity, its power all mesmerized me.

I remember how I would stand, sometimes for hours, in the bathroom at home with the door locked behind me and play the saxophone against the tiles in the shower.

How taken by surprise I would sometimes be by the rich, fat sound as it ricocheted off the tiles and the walls and out of the window, filling me with the most extraordinary feeling of wonder, of connection with myself and the world. How *old* that sound seemed to be—how alive!

Without Merle, it wouldn't have happened.

People who work in great companies—E-Myth Enterprises—think about them in exactly the same way as I think about Merle. It's a love–hate relationship.

An acquaintance of mine who graduated from West Point, earned an MBA from Wharton, and then, as though that weren't enough, completed his sales apprenticeship at IBM, told me that nothing he had ever done in his life measured up to his IBM experience.

"It was the toughest thing I had ever done," he told me proudly. "Without a doubt, no one, nothing has ever tested me as completely as IBM. I loved that place."

A friend of mine who worked intimately with Walt Disney said of him, respectfully, "He was a monster. No one was tougher than Walt. No one expected more of you than Walt. No one rode you as hard, squeezed out the very last juice, kept digging until he found that very last nugget. Once he got it in his mind what he wanted to do, Walt wouldn't let anyone rest until they had done it."

They say the same about Ray Kroc, and Ross Perot, and Fred Smith, and Steve Jobs, and the companies they created. They loved the man and they hated him; they loved the company and they hated it.

So it seems that E-Myth Enterprises—indeed, all companies—take on the personalities of the people who create them.

And that is why so few companies have been successful in their attempt to develop managers into *entrepreneurs.*

It's because personalities like Tom Watson's, Walt Disney's, Ray Kroc's, Ross Perot's, and Steve Jobs's are so uncontrollable. That had to be the reason why Jobs was brought back as Apple's CEO.

They are a force all their own, driven from within, unmanageable, chaotic, solitary, insatiable—possessed, you might say—exactly the opposite of what it takes to be a good manager.

You don't find people like that working in other people's companies for long.

That is why the companies they create demand more of their people than other companies do, because personalities like theirs demand more of *themselves* than other people do.

If my saxophone teacher, Merle, had, by an accident of fate, taken up business instead of the saxophone as his calling, I'm certain his company would have mirrored the ones I've just mentioned. And that is because Merle expected more of himself and more of his students than anyone has a right to expect in the ordinary world.

In the ordinary world, few people have the right to expect to become great saxophone players.

In Merle's world, nothing less would do.

In the ordinary world, few people have the right to expect to create a chain of nearly 32,000 restaurants, all operating in an identical fashion, with the same rigorous standards.

In Ray Kroc's world, nothing less would do.

Companies like these often appear rigid from the outside. That's because they live by rules.

Walt's rules, or Ray's rules, or Tom's rules, or Steve's rules.

Tough rules, rules for a tough world, where ordinary people are unaccustomed to playing.

Despite outward appearances—despite the seeming rigidity of their rules—the truly difficult characteristic of E-Myth Enterprises for ordinary people to take, isn't that they play by the tough rules, *but that they are avid breakers of the very rules they make.*

The rules are constantly changing.

E-Myth Enterprises are continually rewriting their own traditions.

They are continually creating a new game to play.

And that is because the creators of these companies are continually asking questions about how to get better; they are continually rising to their own expectations; they march to the beat of a different drummer. Marching to their own inner tune and living to a measure that comes from just around the corner, out of reach, out of sight, they are continually in a state of breaking up and reforming, and they do this as a matter of being, as a way of life; they couldn't do it any other way.

But their energy, their creativity, their spirit, their drive, their stamina—as essential as these traits are—aren't enough. If they were, there would be many more E-Myth Enterprises than there are.

No, it seems also that E-Myth Entrepreneurs possess, to a degree that puts the rest of us to shame, the five essential skills I spoke about earlier.

They concentrate, discriminate, organize, innovate, and communicate in a way that puts focus, tension, order—a presence—at the heart of the enterprise that causes it to almost shimmer with ecstasy as it goes its unusual way.

It is that *shimmer*, that brightness, that radiance—are these words too strong?—that almost instantly distinguishes an E-Myth Enterprise from all the others, from the inside and from the outside—in the hearts of those people with whom it comes into contact.

It is the fact that game is more important to such

companies than the reward that excites people so much.

But that still is not enough.

There is something else about E-Myth Enterprises that endow them with such a tangible difference. And it is that these businesses, these E-Myth Enterprises, are created, not by businesspeople, not by so-called entrepreneurs, but—and there is no other way to say it—by *children*.

These E-Myth Enterprises are created by the youngest part of us, not the most adult.

They are created by that part of us that believes it has the right to expect the world to change, to give us everything we want, exactly as we imagine it.

Not the methodical part, the dependable part, the reliable part, the responsible part, the grown-up in us all, the part one expects the manager to play.

Not the adult who has learned to limit his or her expectations, but the child who wants it all.

I think of John Anderson, and I immediately know that it was the child in him who created that 1947 Ford coupe.

I think of Merle, and I immediately know that it was the child in him who expected so much to come from my horn. At times, I remember, he would stand beside me with obvious impatience as I was playing my horn and actually stamp his feet, that's right, jump up and down, as if by stamping his feet he could force the sound out of my horn that I was incapable of forcing out myself. He so much wanted to hear that sound!

Who does that but a child?

No wonder there are so few E-Myth Enterprises around.

It's because business, as it is ordinarily played, is so unattractive to most children. It is such a dead and empty game.

Let me tell you the story of another great business—another E-Myth Enterprise.

Let me give you a profound example of how the emotional preferences of people have been so well served, and how this quality alone has enabled one small business to thrive under conditions that would put most businesses under.

Let me tell you the story about a woman named Mary and a vocational school in the field of massage therapy called The Holistic Health Institute.

To Mary Conner Brown, settling down was a color of a different kind. Putting it mildly, she had led a traveler's life. From the moment Mary graduated from the University of North Carolina with a bachelor's in psychology, she hit the road, and for the next five years she rarely stopped in any one place for more than a minute and a half.

As Mary puts it, she wasn't really looking for anything in particular, she was just restless.

She had this burning desire to *do* something, to make

some kind of a mark on the world, to create an impact that would cause people to say, "Mary was here." It took on a physical form, starting, you might say, with her feet—they just wouldn't stop.

Shortly after graduating, Mary heard about, sought out, and immediately joined a commune in Virginia called Twin Trees, which was built on the principles of B. F. Skinner's *Walden Two*. There, Mary alternately worked on the construction team as a plumber, the kitchen team as a cook, and the child care team as a surrogate mother.

Mary remembers the commune as "a powerfully transformational experience."

"It was a true matriarchy, created by women, for women, a place where, for the first time in my life, it became abundantly clear to me that I could damn well do anything I wanted to do.

"Here I was working as a plumber, for God's sake, when just a few months before I couldn't have told you the difference between a pipe wrench and a hammer!

"At Twin Trees, my restlessness—what I thought of at the time as my Search—became focused less on the question of what to do with my life, than on what do I *want* to do with my life?

"The realization that there was a huge difference between those two questions opened up a whole new world to me."

It wasn't long, however, before Mary discovered that, despite its lofty ambitions, Twin Trees had become its own sort of prison, a place so charismatic, so seductive, yet so oppressive, that she knew she had better get out.

As Mary tells it, "It was incredible for me to discover how powerful a hold the commune had on me. The very thing that empowered me there, began to control me. It was like a narcotic. Something in me told me that if I stayed much longer, I would find it difficult, if not impossible, to leave.

"The very next day I literally escaped in a visitor's car by hiding on the floor behind the driver's seat! The guy was shocked to find me there, but agreed to drop me off sixty miles away in Virginia Beach. Why I chose Virginia Beach is still a mystery to me; I think it was the only place that came to mind. It amazes me to this day. In only a couple of hours my entire life had completely changed! Here I was, at three o'clock on a Thursday afternoon, in a strange town, with no identity, no job, no place to live, only $18 to my name, and absolutely no idea of what I was going to do next. I loved it, and I was scared shitless! It was like waking up on a strange planet."

That very afternoon Mary rented a $15 a week room in a boarding hotel and, with only $3 left to her name, began hustling "survival money," doing odd jobs on the streets of Virginia Beach, wondering what the next step in her odyssey would be.

The street became another first for Mary.

Her resilience and resourcefulness were tested over and over again.

Unlike home, college, and the commune, there were no rules on the street, no ritual to which Mary had to conform. No one told her what she had to do, or that she had to do anything.

She made it up as she went along, creating her own rules, her own aims.

Every day became a new opportunity, a new problem. If she was good—or lucky—she got work; if she wasn't, she didn't.

A fast student, she quickly learned the difference between the two. It quickly became a practice. It gave her something of value to teach. She was developing her style.

A company is only as alive as its people.

The vitality of the product of a company, what it sells—its "commodity"—always reflects the emotional vitality of its people.

Put more directly, dumb commodities are created by dumb people.

I think it is also true that commodities mature—become dumber—not only as they outwear their usefulness—for example, their perceived value to their customer—but as the vitality of the people who create them wanes, disintegrates, becomes less intense, less joyful.

On the other hand, the emotional vitality of a company's people is *always* a function of the emotional vitality of the founder, or CEO, of that company.

An old Sicilian expression, "The fish stinks from the head down," tells us where one should look for the failure of a company to thrive.

It's a reliable axiom that dead CEOs create dead companies.

CEOs who are satisfied with themselves create self-satisfied companies.

Dull CEOs create dull companies.

Belligerent CEOs create belligerent companies.

Adventurous CEOs create adventurous companies.

Fearful CEOs create fearful companies.

What goes around comes around.

Most companies fail because there is something missing—some key and critical component left out.

The CEO is adventurous but lazy, so the details don't get worked out.

The CEO is passionate but stupid, so there is force, but in the wrong direction.

The CEO is dissatisfied with himself or herself but places blame on his or her people instead, so "the search" turns into a witch hunt.

Or the CEO is a genius but crazy, so the energy of his or her genius is transformed into a stew pot of confusion.

Consider this: if you want to understand Steve Jobs, look no further than Apple. If you want to understand Howard Schultz, take a good, long look at Starbucks. Conversely, look at Apple to understand Jobs; look at Starbucks to understand Schultz.

What's great about these CEOs is what's great about their companies and vice versa.

This game we call business is a delicate, delicate, yet highly connected thing.

For the next four years, Mary Brown stumbled from one adventure to another, moved more by instinct than anything else.

A stranger on the street got her a job in a beer bar "slinging suds."

A chance encounter in the bar turned into a roommate and a relationship aboard a thirty-five-foot sailboat aptly named *Chance Encounter,* in which she and her new friend sailed to the Bahamas, the Virgin Islands, the Florida Keys, and the Tortugas, working as they went, diving for conch, chartering out, or whatever showed up.

As Mary describes it, "Whatever happened, happened. Something in me craved experience—new impressions. Somehow I knew that the only way I would grow was if I let go of my past and walked willingly into an unknown, an unforeseeable, an uncontrollable future. What's most true of that time in my life is that I simply allowed events to shape me. I was smart enough to know that I didn't know enough to shape events. It's not that I was fear-less, as a lot of people think when I tell them about those times, but that I simply made room for my fear and I established a working relationship with it."

It was during that freewheeling time that Mary's school was born.

Who can say why things happen?

Who can say where anything begins?

But it's instructive to try.

It's of value to look for origins, beginnings, where things begin to go off or on track. For it is undeniable that every single thing, every event, every condition, has its beginning—was started, or was born, or was ignited—at some single point in time. Whether or not we know when, where, or why, it did happen, it did start, and it did come together.

But the most instructive origins are not in the past; they are happening right now.

New things, new ventures, new companies—new *lives*—are continually beginning. At this very instant—in this microsecond, in this flash of contracted time—something new is setting its foot down on a totally new path, is suddenly decided, is charting its course, is cre-ating a future of what will also become past and present events, each existing on the very edge of future instants, future beginnings, and future endings.

It is in the miracle of *occurrence*—this living mo-ment—that everything begins, that everything ends, even businesses, as they have begun, and ended, for all time.

So I think that Tom Peters was wrong.

> It's not the pursuit of excellence that matters, it's
> that we are pursued *by* excellence.
> It's that the question of excellence resides as a pos-
> sibility in everything we do.
> It's not that the gas station is clean that's impor-
> tant, it's that somebody was possessed by the
> need to clean it.
> It's the fire at the heart of life itself, this excellence,
> that either possesses us or not.

And it is this instant that it happens, not in the past, not in the future, but at the very instant of choice, now, as our businesses, as our very lives, are being shaped.

What concerns me, what should concern us all, I think, is how few of us seem to be available—or willing—to be possessed.

It is astonishing to think that Mary's business was started with a book about massage and a handful of clients, both of which (the book and the clients) were given to Mary by a massage therapy friend who decided to leave town.

Mary read the book and massaged the clients, and thus her school was born.

How Mary Brown came upon the idea for her school isn't important. You couldn't replicate it even if you wanted to. The simple matter is that she was passionately seeking something, and she found it.

Don't misunderstand me, it wasn't the school she was seeking—the business never is, not for Disney, not for Kroc, not for Smith, not for Perot, not for Jobs, not for Mary. No, the business is simply the medium through which such people hope to find what they're looking for.

For Mary Brown, the school was, and still is, a mirror—a reflection of her true self.

She sees herself in it every single day.
It is a product of who she is.
It is a continuing commentary on what she has learned, and on what she hasn't.
It is—like the streets of Virginia Beach—a difficult place to go to sleep.

Several years ago, Mary, like all the other owners of vocational schools with student aid programs in her state, was peremptorily notified by the state that the rules for such schools were about to be changed.

Changed, however, is too mild a word for what the state had in mind.

What the state had in mind was a revolution.

This revolution was going to take place immediately,

and anyone who didn't comply immediately with the state's new rules would be found in violation and could be put out of business.

The state had decided to create a new game, a game called "Try this one on for size."

Just a few examples:

What the state said was that such schools could no longer pay their sales staff commissions for enrollments until the students they enrolled graduated from school, forcing schools to create a totally new compensation system for their salespeople (at great additional expense to the school) and take the risk of losing all their sales staff at the same time.

The state didn't care.

What the state said was that any student on financial aid had the right to drop out of school at any time and receive a full pro rata refund of his or her unearned tuition, forcing schools to rethink their entire financial strategy, their capital requirements, their financial aid programs—without any data to support their conclusions.

The state didn't care.

What the state said was that the school had to guarantee that at least 70 percent of its graduating students would be fully employed in the field for which they were trained within six months of graduating, or the school would be in default.

Can you imagine what would happen to state universities and colleges if the same rules applied to them?

That all psychology students who had received financial aid had to be employed as psychologists within six months of graduation; that all music students who had received financial aid had to be employed as musicians within six months of graduation; that all teaching students who had received financial aid had to be employed as teachers within six months of graduation, and that all engineering students who had received financial aid had to be employed as engineers within six months of graduation?

Do you suppose state schools could survive under those rules?

Could your business?

What if the state required you to guarantee your product or service?

What if the state demanded that you provide your people with a guarantee of success when you hire them?

What if the state told you how much capital your business needed to have in relationship to your revenue in order for you to be permitted to stay in business?

What if the state told you what your net profit needed to be in order for you to be permitted to stay in business?

What if the state told you what you could say, and what you couldn't say, to your customers in your marketing process in order for you to be permitted to stay in business?

Well, the state said these things, and much more, to the vocational schools doing business there. But what the state didn't say was how it came to these brilliant conclusions.

Instead, what the state did was to shove dozens of small vocational schools to the very brink of financial disaster and put many others out of business.

As you might imagine, most of the schools, small and large, were simply unprepared and therefore unable to comply.

But on the very day when all schools were expected to be in compliance, *with only two weeks' notice*, Mary's school had fulfilled every single requirement imposed on it.

She had done the impossible in record time.

Mary was able to accomplish the impossible in record time because her school possessed something few businesses possess: the people who worked for her, bought from her, sold to her, and loaned her money loved her and the school she had created.

They thought she was incredible, and, the simple truth of it is, they were right.

Mary had created a wonder out of nothing.

Her school was started in a small, shabby house with

six students, no capital, and absolutely no business experience of any kind. But she knew about people and what it took to survive on the streets.

More importantly, she knew that she wanted to teach her students more than a skill. She wanted to teach them what she had learned, and she wanted to teach them what she hadn't.

She wanted to teach people that it was possible to have work they love and to have it on their own terms.

But she also wanted to teach people what it takes to make it on their own—to become independent of the system, to grow, and expand, and thrive, as she had, to take risks, as she had, to test themselves, as she had—without any certainty, or any guarantee whatsoever that the end would justify the means.

Mary was afire with her convictions and absolutely inspired by what she had to do.

And what she was about to do was learn.

■

There are seven rules Mary learned about building an emotionally vital business.

The first rule Mary learned is that people need order. They need to know that there is a structure, a logic, a foundation, a clear set of standards, of principles, a fairness about the business and the job they are there to do.

The second rule Mary learned is that people need to feel heard. They need to know that their contribution is important, that no matter where they stand in relationship to the business—as employee, as customer, as supplier, as lender—what they want matters, and that there is a channel through which they can express what matters to them, and that the channel is always open.

The third rule Mary learned is that people need to feel connected to something bigger than themselves. If the business has small aims, is simply interested in surviving, in staying in business, it will not sustain them, it will not touch them, it will not engage them. No, the business has to take on something—*no matter what kind of a business it is*—in an important way. It has to be willing to tilt at windmills—the bigger, the better.

People are dying for want of something larger than life to believe in, to rally around, to support. Could that be why young men and women volunteer to serve in the armed forces, even in times of war or unrest?

The fourth rule Mary learned is that people need to have a purpose. They need to have a plan. They need to be going someplace—someplace specific, in a specific amount of time. Without a purpose, people begin to wallow. They become suspended in time. They become a drag on each other, begin to feel victimized, lose track of the time, go to movies and forget what they've seen.

The fifth rule Mary learned is that people need to feel that what they are doing has moral weight. The business has to be concerned about what is right: what is right for themselves, what is right for others, and what is right for the world. The business has to operate with *conscience*. Without conscience, a business is a drag on what little self-esteem people already possess.

The sixth rule Mary learned is that people need to feel that what they personally do is important. They need to feel that the enterprise, without them, somehow wouldn't matter as much; that when they walk in the door, something vital is added to the business, something only they can bring to the table. They need to feel that if they were no longer there, the business wouldn't be the same.

The seventh rule Mary learned about the emotional health of a business is that people need to feel that the people they associate with love them. That, no matter what, people care.

The words a student of Mary Brown's wrote express it all:

> *Mary C. Brown, what a lady!*
> *She beats my brain out daily.*
> *She's rough, she's tough,*
> *But she knows her stuff.*
> *(And she can charm the socks off a baby!)*
> *I love you, Mary C. Brown!*

* * *

DESIGNING THE ENTERPRISE:
THE TAKEAWAY POINTS

(Listen to the Podcast version
at MichaelEGerber.com)

■

The second category of preference is the emotional ideal. There are seven rules that will help you build an emotionally vital enterprise.

1. **People need order.** They need to know that there is a structure, a logic, a foundation, a clear set of standards, of principles, a fairness about the business and the job they are there to do.

2. **People need to feel heard.** They need to know that their contribution is important, that no matter where they stand in relationship to the business— as employees, as customers, as suppliers, as lenders—what they want matters, that there is a channel through which they can express what matters to them, and that the channel is always open.

3. **People need to feel connected to something bigger than themselves.** If the business has small aims, is

simply interested in surviving, in staying in business, it will not sustain them, it will not touch
them, it will not engage them. No, the business has
to take on something—*no matter what kind of a
business it is*—in an important way.

4. **People need to have a purpose.** They need to
have a plan. They need to be going someplace—
someplace specific, in a specific amount of time.
Without a purpose, people begin to wallow. They
become suspended in time. They become a drag on
each other, begin to feel victimized, and lose track
of the time.

5. **People need to feel that what they are doing has
moral weight.** The business has to be concerned
about what is right: what is right for themselves,
what is right for others, and what is right for the
world. The business has to operate with *conscience.*
Without conscience, a business is a drag on what
little self-esteem people already possess.

6. **People need to feel that what they personally do
is important.** They need to feel that the enterprise,
without them, somehow wouldn't matter as much;
that when they walk in the door, something vital
is added to the business, something only they can
bring to the table. They need to feel that if they

were no longer there, the business wouldn't be the same.

7. **People need to feel that the people they associate with love them.** That, no matter what, people care.

   Some of you might argue that the emotional ideal is not as important as great products, great services, and competent management. Trust me, it is at least as important.

* * *

CHAPTER SIX

THE THIRD CATEGORY
OF PREFERENCE:
THE FUNCTIONAL IDEAL

◼

**I've noticed that people who have
never worked with steel have trouble
seeing this . . . that the motorcycle is primarily
a mental phenomenon.**

—Robert M. Pirsig,
*Zen and the Art of
Motorcycle Maintenance*

That a company looks great and feels great is still insufficient for a company to act great. For a company to act great, it must think in a significantly different way about what it does and how it does it than most companies are prepared to do. That is because most companies are people-oriented rather than process-oriented.

People-oriented companies focus their attention on who is doing the work.

Process-oriented companies focus their attention on whether the right work is being done, and more importantly, if the right work is being done, how it is being done.

People-oriented companies depend on "good" people to produce results, where *good* is defined as experienced, successful, self-motivated—in short, people who can be depended upon to produce good results. Someone is always shouting, "Find me someone who knows how to get the job done!" in a people-oriented company.

Process-oriented companies depend on good processes to produce results, where good is defined as the process's ability to produce the very best results in the hands of inexperienced (or less experienced) people than the competition needs to produce the same results.

It's valuable to note that most of the people-oriented companies I have known (and I have known thousands of them) are almost always intolerably self-righteous about their great people orientation ("We're a people company!"), when in fact they are usually far less people-oriented than they would have us believe.

When something goes wrong in a people-oriented business, someone invariably asks the question "What's wrong with Jack?"

(It's a sine qua non that in people-oriented companies, somebody's always letting the company down. If the definition of good people is people who produce good results, logic would tell us that when people fail to produce good results, they're not good people. Not a cheery position to be in.)

When something goes wrong in a true process-oriented company, the question that invariably is asked first is "What's wrong with the process?"

("Jack" isn't the problem; the process is.)

One might argue, "Ah, yes, but who creates the process in the first place but 'good' people?"

And I would respond, "People using a process!"

A people-oriented company's strategy is almost always different than a process-oriented company's strategy.

A people-oriented company first looks for the best person for the job—somebody who already knows how to do it, has done it very successfully in the past, and is self-motivated to do it.

Should such a person be found, the people-oriented company will most often provide the new person with an "orientation," a generalized review of housekeeping principles—"This is where you get the grease; this is where we keep the pencils; this is where you can buy some coffee; this is Fred; this is Jocko; this is Myrtle"—then leaves the new person to get on with what the company hired him or her to do, to find his or her own way, to do the job the best way he or she can.

Failing to find the best person, a people-oriented company will resort to teaching as "good" a person as it can find the skills needed to perform effectively on the job, then show him or her where the grease is, where the pencils are, where he or she can buy some coffee, this is Fred, this is Jocko, this is Myrtle, and finally give the new person "the room" to decide how he or she prefers to do the job.

(Skills must be differentiated here from process, in that skills, as they are commonly taught in people-oriented companies, are those basic abilities used by all companies of the same category—for example, all auto repair shops, or all poodle-clipping shops, or all insurance companies—to get the job done in an undifferentiated way. Process-oriented companies, in contrast, design processes that are unique to their company so as to get the job done in a way that preferentially differentiates that company from its competitors—faster, smoother, less expensive, with a unique flourish.)

Process-oriented companies know that the discovery of a better way to do something is significantly more empowering than finding a better person to do it.

Process-oriented companies know that you can always lose the better person (indeed, in this day and age, you always do!), but that it's much more difficult to lose a better process. (People aren't the exclusive property of your company, but your processes can be.)

In short, process-oriented companies know that a better process can be liberating in that it has the power of turning ordinary people into extraordinary people. (The best people can be a limiting factor, in that there are so few of them, you have to pay a premium to get them. Once you do get them, they can hold you for ransom if they decide they're bored with the present arrangement. Or if it's just not quite right today. Or if they need a vacation you hadn't planned for. Or for any reason—of theirs—at all. Then try to *replace* them.)

Now, I know that if you're what would be categorized on the job as a "best person" this whole concept may offend you, and I apologize for the offense, but the good news is that a great process in the hands of a great person is a wonder to behold.

Witness *Hamlet* and Laurence Olivier.

Witness Beethoven's Fifth Symphony and Leonard Bernstein.

Witness Eric Clapton and a well-tuned guitar.

Witness Brett Favre, or Tom Brady, or Peyton Manning and a football.

Witness a star at anything, and you'll understand what I mean.

Every great person uses a great process.

The question here is, who owns the process?

For a process to be liberating, it must liberate everyone—the employees, the customers, the suppliers, and the lenders.

Such process-oriented companies as Supercuts, Lens-

Crafters, Pizza Hut, Subway—and, of course, McDonald's, the Walt Disney Company, Apple, and FedEx—and many, many more, all produce liberating results for their employees, their customers, their suppliers, and their lenders.

The process assures all of them a measure of predictability that few businesses produce for *anyone*, let alone for all four.

Supercuts possesses a process for cutting hair that enables a beginner to produce a professional result in short order at half the price a professional must charge.

LensCrafters possesses a process for creating quality eyeglasses "in about an hour" for people who simply can't, or don't want to, wait any longer.

FedEx possesses a process that virtually guarantees satisfied customers with its amazing record of reliability and its willingness to make the delivery, no matter what.

All differentiate themselves not by the people who work for them, but by the process through which these people produce a predictable result each and every time.

And because they possess a process that works, their people are perceived to work better than most.

Think about it this way: there is a way to do everything.

And if that is true, then there must be a better way to do everything.

And if that is true, then there must be a best way to do everything.

Not the only way, mind you, not absolutely and forever the best way. But the relatively best way, the way that produces the best results as perceived by the people with whom it interacts, the way that performs best in relationship to all the other options available at this time and for the foreseeable future.

That is what process-oriented companies are all about, discovering the best way.

But where they start is not with how to do it, but with the question "What is the best thing to do?"

And the question "What is the best thing to do?" can only be answered by understanding what people want most.

A best way process is discovered by answering the following questions:

What one thing would our customers, employees, suppliers, and lenders most like us to do for them that we and our competitors can't currently do?

Has anyone ever tried to do this thing?

If yes, why did they fail?

What would it mean to us if we could do it?

Why can't we do it?

What would be the best way to do it?

How much would it cost us to be able to do it the best way?

Is it worth the cost?

If yes, what would be the impact on our customers, employees, suppliers, and lenders?

If negative for any or all, how would we overcome
that negative?

If we can't overcome the negative, do the benefits
outweigh the negative aspects?

If we can, should we do it?

The best way is always the way that eliminates the
primary frustration experienced by any one of the four
primary influencers of a business.

■

What is the primary frustration?

Just what you might think.

* * *

The primary frustration is the negative experience most commonly complained about concerning someone's interaction with a business.

It's not difficult to find out what the primary frustration is.

For example, ask a hundred people who have done business with a building contractor about the transaction, and at least seventy-five will say, "The job wasn't completed when they said it would be; there was always an excuse."

Ask a hundred people who have had their auto repaired about the transaction, and at least eighty will say, "I felt totally out of control, and they make me feel worse."

Ask a hundred people who have been to a doctor about the transaction, and at least ninety will say, "I waited too long to see the doctor!"

Stereotypes? True. But it is in these stereotypical responses that one finds the primary frustration and the best way.

What would happen to the general contractor who says, "At Heartfelt Construction, we are always on time, on price, and deliver a spotless performance—or we pay for it! Guaranteed!"

What would happen to the auto repair shop that says, "When something goes wrong with your car, the one thing you don't need is more worry. At Hearthstone Auto, you'll always have a good experience—or the job is on us. Guaranteed!"

What would happen to the medical office that says, "At Sweet Water Medical Office, we always keep our appointments on time—or we pay for the visit. Guaranteed!"

What would happen if they actually did these things?

If they actually pulled off those guarantees?

If they eliminated, once and for all, the primary frustration normally experienced by most people who interact with their kinds of businesses day after day?

If they were to set their attention on it until their businesses became masters at performing the impossible?

Wouldn't that make a difference to the people who buy from them, the people who work for them, the people who sell to them, and the people who lend to them?

Wouldn't that have a positive impact on everyone involved?

Wouldn't that set their business apart?

Isn't that obvious?

Well, that's what process-oriented companies are all about: inventing an unobvious way to do the obvious, every single time.

■

**To make a promise—and to accept full
responsibility for the delivery
of that promise—requires control, the kind
of control that only a process-oriented
company can hope to exercise.**

* * *

Let me tell you about just such a company, Santos Construction, a small business that determined what the primary frustration of their customers was and decided to do something bold about it.

Marino Santos used to wear black to work every day, except for a bright red scarf he wore as a sweatband that also served to tie back his crow-black hair.

Marino Santos loved the color black. To him, black signified mastery, singleness of purpose, seriousness, and also danger. Black was the color by which Marino Santos marked the barriers that distinguished him, and therefore separated him, from the rest of the world. Black warned the world that Marino Santos was a serious fellow, not to be fooled with. Black was his shield.

On the other hand, red was the color of Marino Santos's heart.

His bright red scarf signified to Marino Santos the passion of his interest. It was the hot, restless flame at the center of his life, the intense fire that burned inside him, inside the black container, the cold shield of his distance.

While his black clothes said, "I stand alone," his red scarf said, "I'm about to explode!"

And explode he did, every day at work. It was in the nature of the work that he did.

Marino Santos was what is called in the construction trade a framer. He and his small crew subcontracted the framing of homes in Southern California, Arizona, Nevada, Colorado—wherever the work was.

To the general contractors who hired them, they were simply known as Santos's crew. Inside the small company, however—more like a small band of men than an actual business—they thought of themselves as *los apasionados sin igual*—"the only ones."

Everyone in the trade knew Santos's crew. Among their peers, Marino Santos and his band were the stuff of folklore. It was not only that they were the best at what they did—and there was no doubt in anyone's mind that they were—but there was the mystique, the machismo, that accompanied them everywhere they went.

Like the stars they were, Santos's crew remained aloof. At breaks, they would gather together, seated in a small, tight circle on a concrete slab facing each other while they quietly drank their coffee, ate their burritos, and whispered among themselves—star talk, no one knew about what.

But when Marino Santos and his crew went to work, there was nothing quiet about them at all. Their framing hammers fairly flew! Walls went up in record time—first one house, then another, emerging as though miraculously from the concrete slabs. You could literally watch the houses grow, they went up so fast. Marino Santos was in the middle of it all, his muscular arm with its shining blue steel hammer, as if growing out of his hand, whaling away at the wood, thwack, thwack, thwack; his strong melodic voice leading the songs, calling out names, swearing at the sky.

And they did it to music! For Marino Santos's crew, every day on the job was a performance, a dance, a physical and visual crusade. *Los apasionados sin igual*—"the only ones." It was what they did. It was their signature. It was what they were known for. It was what they lived to do. It was who they were.

Then, early one Wednesday morning in the middle of July, on the way to a job in Barstow, Marino Santos's pickup blew a tire and flew off the road at ninety miles an hour and turned over five times until it finally came to rest upside down against a boulder. For thirteen hours, Marino Santos lay trapped in his truck with a broken back before he was finally discovered by the Highway Patrol.

That he survived the accident was a miracle.

But he was out of the framing business for good.

What does a framer do when he can't frame anymore, especially when he's a man like Marino Santos?

What does a star do when the very thing at which he excels is suddenly taken away from him?

What does a man who uses his body for a living do when his body can no longer perform?

What does a company do when it has built its ability to perform on the skills of a handful of good people and they're suddenly gone?

For the first six months or so, Marino Santos did little or nothing but drink. He woke up in the morning and drank, and he didn't stop until he passed out at night.

At times he would get so furious with his condition that he would heave an empty whiskey bottle through the closed bedroom window and into the street, then sit there in his wheelchair amid the shards of broken glass, screaming into the night at anyone who would listen. The police would come by, but they wouldn't do anything other than threaten to take him in.

His crew came to visit him every day. They hated to see him like he was. They called him names. They cried with him. They sat silently by and said nothing. They threatened that they wouldn't come back anymore. They played music and drank with him. They did whatever they could for both him and themselves—sometimes just to be there was enough.

And then, as suddenly as it began, it was over.

One day he seemed just as bad, and the next day he was better.

He called his crew together.

"I want to apologize to all of you," he said.

"Not for the past six months, not for the drinking—I couldn't help that.

"I want to apologize for the framing, for the arrogance, for the belief I had in my body, for being so stupid.

"I don't want to be stupid anymore," Marino Santos said.

"It's time to start a new business."

Marino Santos didn't care what his new business was, although he knew it would have something to do with construction. Construction was in his blood. He loved the smell of raw wood. He loved seeing things start from nothing and become something almost overnight. He loved the physical impact it had on the world. It was a mark of his having been there. It was something you could touch and look at for years after.

Yes, it had to be construction, but other than that it didn't matter what kind of construction it was.

Except for this: the construction his new business did was going to have as profound an impact on the people around him as his old business did, except that the new business would not depend on his, or his crew's, physical skills. The business would work without them.

At first his men didn't understand. They had always

worked with their bodies. They had always taken pride in their extraordinary physical skill. Not to work like that anymore didn't make sense. Their joy was to express themselves physically, to move on the concrete slab, to raise walls, to walk the rafters. To think of not doing these things anymore created great sadness in all of them.

But because they cared for and respected Marino Santos so much, they listened. And gradually, it came to them that what Marino Santos was talking about wouldn't deprive them of anything, but would give them something they had never had.

In one of their many conversations together, Marino Santos said, "I have thought about this a good deal. It comes down to this: either we work for a living, like *burros*, until we can't work anymore (he spread his arms as if to say, "I am the proof"), or we find a way to build a business that works for us. We *think* about this business, we put our minds to it; we shape it so that it works like we have learned to work, with precision, with joy, with energy. But we must find a way to do this without people like us, people like us who take pride in being separate from the world, people like us who need to be alone. People like us will eventually kill our business, as I have almost killed our business. No, we must build a business that can make it easy for people who are not like us, and who will never be like us, to act like us. It is our fierce pride that makes us so good. We must learn how to give this fierce pride to people who do not possess it naturally.

We must make it possible for everyone who works in our business to become as good as we are as long as they work in our business. That will be our gift to them. We must find a way to do this.

"Our business will give them something they can't get elsewhere in the world. And, as a result of that, they will stay, and our business will flourish. That will be their gift to us. Those who are like us, however, the other *los apasionados sin igual* in the world, must do what they must do. There is nothing we can do for them."

As always, once they made their mind up, Marino Santos and his crew took their path seriously.

In accordance with Marino Santos's instructions, each man took it as his personal mission to find work in some segment of the construction industry that was new to him.

They segmented the industry into new construction and reconstruction, and into commercial and residential. They then broke each segment into parts, to find out which segment and which part of that segment was most promising as a business opportunity.

Marino Santos told them that time was not important. What was important was making certain of their ultimate selection—that it be the single segment of the construction industry that could provide them with the greatest opportunity to achieve their objective.

It had to be a segment of the industry that had a consistent growth pattern, did not experience sharp up-

and-down swings because of the economy, was relatively compartmentalized—that is, repeated the same tasks much the same way from job to job—wasn't capital intensive to either start or maintain, and could be operated independently of other contractors—that is, could secure, start, and complete a contract without having to depend on subcontractors or general contractors to do their parts of the job.

Marino Santos's kitchen served as their operations center.

Every night after work, the men reported their findings over a cold beer.

There were heated arguments. Each man came to conclusions that others refuted. But gradually, as the men became smarter about their mission, more intelligent about their conclusions, and more eloquent in the positions each took, their arguments became less heated, though no less intense.

Marino Santos's strategy was simple: as one industry segment after another was excluded as an option, the men who were employed in those segments would leave them to find work in the remaining segments, until finally they would all be working in the same industry segment—the segment of choice—but for competing contractors.

And that's exactly what happened.

After two and a half years of dedicated work, research, and planning, Marino Santos and his men found themselves decided.

It was such a simple, uncomplicated decision when they finally came to it.

They would go into the kitchen remodeling business.

And they would call it Three Day Kitchens.

On the face of it, there is something so ordinary about business.

Something so unimportant, so trivial.

For Marino Santos and his men to apply themselves so determinedly, to expend so much effort and time to the ordinary task of deciding what business to go into, to spend all that energy merely to start a kitchen remodeling business, when instead they could have done . . . what?

What also would a man like Marino Santos do? Join the Peace Corps? Graduate from MIT or Stanford? Enter a monastery? Try out for the Olympics? Write a book?

What better could any of us do than he?

How many people do you know who have expended as much effort, intelligence, care, or attention on the selection of a path?

How many people do you know who have taken such a passionate interest in every single thing they do?

How many people do you know who could remember their aim for as long as two and a half years with only their own interest to remind them of it, who could bring the energy and attention of a group of strong-willed people to bear down on a problem that had no end in sight, and still maintain that energy and attention as well as Marino Santos did, and who could keep that attention from wavering, from getting lost among the daily concerns that plague us all, and certainly must have plagued him?

Who do you know who possesses such force of purpose, such impeccable will?

What difference does it make what the business is, after all?

Or that it is a business?

These men—these *apasionados sin igual*—could have been climbing the Himalayas, and it wouldn't have added one thing to their journey.

In fact, it was at least two more years before Marino Santos and his men completed their first kitchen for pay. They installed hundreds of kitchens for practice. Every conceivable problem was faced, agonized over, dealt with, and overcome.

They worked at night and on weekends in a warehouse Marino Santos rented, in which they constructed dozens of practice kitchen sites. Every kitchen problem his men faced during their day on the job was put on paper at night and analyzed, scrutinized, discussed, argued about, until every peculiarity, every exception, every unpredictable variable faced in the kitchen remodeling business had been reviewed at least a dozen times—and sometimes even more often than that—looking for the similarities, the predictable, the standardizing opportunities.

No one, they were sure, had ever spent as much time,

trouble, and intelligence to solve the problems associated with kitchen remodeling.

They were determined to get it right.

They were going to create a kitchen remodeling system such as the world had never seen, that could produce an absolutely predictable result in the hands of novice workers trained only in their system, and they were going to figure out how to do it—how to completely renovate and remodel any kitchen—walls, windows, floors, cabinets, lighting, plumbing—all within no more than three days. Guaranteed!

And they were going to figure out how to do it at a cost significantly below the competition, at a quality significantly better than any one around, and at a profit that would justify it being done at all.

The competition, Marino Santos discovered (though he wasn't surprised), was not the problem. There was no competition. Not for the company he intended to create.

His men reported daily on the waste, inefficiency, lack of skill, disinterest, and lack of management on the jobs they were working.

Materials and men rarely showed up on time, and sometimes never.

The job site was usually a mess.

"They are pigs," one of his men reported disdainfully.

Where heavy reconstruction was required and surprises were discovered (as they often were), the job could be delayed for hours, even days, until the almost always absent contractor, or his foreman, if he had one, showed up to personally solve the problem.

No, as Marino Santos knew only so well, contractors were not fastidious men.

Shoddy work was normal; there was no training.

Experienced people were either hired out of the hall, off the street, or as subcontractors. The margins were so thin that there was no time or money, nor people to spend on developing new people.

No, other contractors would not determine Three Day Kitchens' success or failure. He and his men would.

They worked like they had never worked before. They were determined to get it right.

A kitchen, more than any other room in a house, is built to certain predictable standards.

Approached randomly, that is, without a database of quantified experience, it might seem that every kitchen presents a unique problem—that every one is different. This is not the case.

Unfortunately, few small remodeling contractors have ever quantified any of their experience, and so what they find themselves dealing with day in and day out are seemingly uncommon, or problematic, conditions that always call for uncommon and, usually, costly reactions.

Indeed, what Marino Santos and his crew discovered is that most of the kitchen work they monitored over the two years of the study was predictably and monotonously the same, presenting measurably few variations on a repetitious theme.

Therefore, to invent a kitchen remodeling system that could guarantee an installed kitchen in exactly three days meant only that Marino Santos and his men had to determine what those variations on the theme were; create a variety of preplanned kitchen solutions to address each and every one of them; design a preprogrammed construction and installation strategy for each kitchen solution; recruit, hire, and then rigorously train a small crew of inexperienced technicians in their construction and installation system; and establish a management system that would assure Marino Santos and his men that their system would be used exactly as planned, each and every time.

And then, practice, practice, practice these processes, over and over and over again, until there wasn't a question in anyone's mind that they could be implemented faithfully and impeccably every single time.

Marino Santos and his men boiled their mission down to five essential ingredients:

1. Control what is sold.
2. Control how it is sold.
3. Control how it is planned.
4. Control how it is built and installed.
5. Control how it is monitored.

The failure of a contractor to exercise control over any

one of these five control points, as Marino Santos and his men referred to them, meant that the job wouldn't be completed as promised.

That would not be a problem at Three Day Kitchens.

They renewed their intention each day.

The night following their first paid kitchen installment was a special night for Marino Santos and his men. It had gone off without a hitch, but they had known it would turn out that way long before the job began.

They had planned it that way, and they had practiced their process diligently. Nothing was taken for granted.

Their customer was astonished.

Not only was the job done exactly as promised, but the men who did it were astonishingly clean, well organized, and fastidious in their comportment—"joyful," the customer said, expressing her delight to Marino Santos about not only having the job done exactly as promised, but having experienced people who obviously loved their work so well.

"How do you find such good people?" she asked.

Marino Santos smiled. "I wish I knew," he said.

* * *

DESIGNING THE ENTERPRISE: THE TAKEAWAY POINTS

**(Listen to the Podcast version
at MichaelEGerber.com)**

■

The third category of preference is the functional ideal.

The underlying question always is, What is the best thing to do? That can only be answered by understanding what people want most.

The "best way process" is discovered by answering the following questions:

- What one thing would our customers, employees, suppliers, and lenders most like us to do for them that we and our competitors can't currently do?
- Has anyone ever tried to do this thing?
- If yes, why did they fail?
- What would it mean to us if we could do it?
- Why can't we do it?
- What would be the best way to do it?
- How much would it cost us to be able to do it the best way?
- Is it worth the cost?

- If yes, what would be the impact on our customers, employees, suppliers, and lenders?
- If negative for any or all, how would we overcome that negative?
- If we can't overcome the negative, do the benefits outweigh the negative aspects?
- If we can, should we do it?

The best way is always the way that eliminates the primary frustration experienced by any one of the four primary influencers of a business.

The primary frustration is the negative experience most commonly complained about concerning someone's interaction with a business.

Thus, to become the functional ideal, you must eliminate the primary frustration experienced by any one of the four primary influencers of a business.

* * *

CHAPTER SEVEN

THE FOURTH CATEGORY
OF PREFERENCE:
THE FINANCIAL IDEAL

■

Money, money, money. They're driving me crazy!

—Anonymous CEO

I'm going to change the tone right now.

I have to tell you something truly important.

I need to talk about money.

The most important thing I have learned is that we don't spend money as much as we consume it. Money is food.

We consume it and convert it into things—the feelings, associations, and symbols we believe in.

That's what a consumer society really means. It takes the material idea of money, ingests it, digests it, and converts it into its idea of living.

To some, money is converted into power.

To others, money is converted into security.

To others, money is converted into getting by the best way they can.

To others, money is converted into self-esteem.

To others, money is converted into survival.

To others, money is converted into scarcity.

To others, money is converted into magic.

To others, sex.

To still others, beauty.

To many, money is converted into sin.

And to still others, money is converted into evil.

The fact is that money does not exist without people.

Money has no meaning without people.

Money is simply an idea we have agreed upon, an idea that represents to every one of us our net worth in the world.

A word about money.

I have heard so many New Age would-be business mavens repeat that saddest of noxious platitudes, "Do the right things, and the money will take care of itself." Let me tell you this: the money *never* takes care of itself. *Never.*

YOU have to take care of money.

Daily.

Not monthly, not annually, but daily.

By the hour is best.

I have learned that everyone has a different perception of money—ingests money, digests money, values money—in a totally subjective and very personal way. Employees. Customers. Suppliers. Lenders.

Don't screw around with those perceptions!

You will lose a hand!

And if you persist, you'll lose more than that.

In a free market system, money is the measure.

In a free market system, money speaks.

In a free market system, we have been taught only too well that what we own is who we are, and what we own is the by-product of money.

Don't mess with that truth.

Don't even think you can mess with that truth.

The minute you mess with that truth, no matter what you believe to be true about the person whose money you're messing around with, that person will have your head.

He won't intend to, mind you.

He wouldn't believe it of himself.

But he will do it all the same!

He will eat your head for lunch!

Please don't call me cynical. I'm not.

Please don't send me e-mails proving me wrong, or that you have an example of how wrong I can be.

Please don't bother; I'm sure there are exceptions to the rule. There always are.

But the rule is the rule nonetheless.

Mess around with people's money in a free market system, and your goose is cooked.

Even if you didn't do it, they'll say you did.

Even if you did do it but didn't intend to, your name is still mud.

Even if you only thought about doing it, the wrath will descend upon you as though from the hand of God.

In a free market system, money is a monstrously complicated thing.

It is all some people have.

It is all some people are.

It is all some people want.

It is what lies down beside them in bed at night.

It is how they value their day.

If they think they have a right to it, they will kill you for it.

If they think that they are in danger of losing what they have, they will buy a handgun and run away to the hills to protect it.

If they believe it is sexy, they will make love to it.

If they believe it is power, they will make a club of it and beat you senseless until you submit.

If they believe it will keep them safe, they will dress themselves in it.

In a free market system, money is the only thing that

stands between most people and the awful, bottomless, terrifying void.

I learned about money in the most difficult way, almost losing my business once and for all in 1985. Having my ass sued off by "evildoers." Spending years to pay off $2 million in debt.

I could have followed the easy path. I could have gone bankrupt. In fact, that's what was suggested by my most trusted advisers and highly paid consultants I brought in to fix the mess I unexpectedly, inexplicably found myself in. But I didn't. I stayed the course. I'm glad I did.

Because, while money is everything . . . money *isn't* everything. Trust me. Your word, your integrity, is everything.

* * *

DESIGNING THE ENTERPRISE:
THE TAKEAWAY POINTS

**(Listen to the Podcast version
at MichaelEGerber.com)**

■

The fourth category of preference is the financial ideal.

You've heard the platitude, "Do the right things, and the money will take care of itself"? Let me tell you this: the money *never* takes care of itself. *Never.*

YOU have to take care of money. Daily.

In a free market system, money is the measure. Money speaks.

Don't mess with that truth. The minute you mess with that truth, no matter what you believe to be true about the person whose money you're messing around with, that person will have your head.

To become the financial ideal, you must have integrity when it comes to money. Your investors, your bankers, your accountants, your suppliers, your customers, and your employees must know, without a doubt, that you have integrity. You back up your word with compatible actions.

Money can be your ally and help you build your business. Or it can be your enemy and destroy your business. The decision belongs to you.

* * *

CHAPTER EIGHT

THE E-MYTH PERSPECTIVE

■

**Consciousness and Conscience are similar
in their respective spheres, one being in the
Intellectual Center, the other in the Emotional
Center. Consciousness is Knowing all together;
Conscience is Feeling all together.**

—Maurice Nicoll,
Psychological Commentaries

I'm sure that countless businesses in this country have
responded enthusiastically over the past several years to
the clarion call for a return to those worthwhile puri-
tan values of *service, excellence,* and *caring.* To the creation of "vision statements" and "mission statements,"
and "values," and the nurturing of their "corporate
culture."

You know who you are.

Unfortunately, I'm also sure that, despite the initial fervor such clarion calls create, most of these businesses operate the same way today as they did before the flag was raised, with equally slipshod service, mediocre performance, and as greedy and self-serving a mind-set as ever.

That's because neither service, excellence, nor caring can be produced by executive fiat, or by wishing it so.

Tom Peters and other such gurus can rail all they want. It won't make any difference.

The adoption of service, excellence, and caring as strategic options—as slogans—to revive a dead or dying business is not only antithetical to the true meaning of those words, but as cynical as anything our Machiavellian minds can produce. In short, it won't work.

Service, excellence, and caring are not something you can do anything about. They are a state of mind.

When a business is bereft of such qualities, it is because its founders, its owners, and its managers are bereft of such qualities.

They don't care to serve.
It doesn't bother them that their performance is
    less, by far, than excellent.
They don't care about the business because they
    simply don't care at all.

That's why such words fail to work for them, indeed

for most companies that attempt to adopt them for their own purposes, to their own strategic ends.

Because the cynical use of true human values always produces exactly the opposite of what was intended.

True human values cannot be adopted for the expedient or the pragmatic. They are not "tools" with which to develop a "management style."

They are *values*. They are beliefs. They are how one views the world. They are either a part of us, or they're not.

They cannot be tried on like a suit, the right color, the right shape. They are not there to be used. They can't be. They won't tolerate it. There is something fundamentally obscene about even trying to.

So, to create an E-Myth Enterprise, you—the founders, the owners, and the managers of companies everywhere—must already possess an E-Myth Perspective.

And if you don't already have one, you're in deep, deep trouble.

Those who possess an E-Myth Perspective are what I would call pragmatic idealists. They are never happy with anything less than perfection, but they measure perfection by its unparalleled ability to produce practical results in the world.

Pragmatic idealists are not sentimental.

They are driven.

They are not patient.

They are often unkind.

Pragmatic idealists do not pander to the comfort zone in people. They do not make it easy for people to get by.

My saxophone teacher was a pragmatic idealist. He lived in a world of perfection, but he practiced achieving it in this world. He could hear the perfect tone in his head. He could imagine the perfect scale.

I doubt that he ever was satisfied, however, with any of his students, or with himself. Yet he loved what he did and what they did. It was his passion and his paradox.

He would listen to Charlie Parker with awe, yet he could hear every flaw, every inarticulate statement, every failure to touch the sublime, the perfect, the absolute.

And as much as he held Charlie Parker in awe, Merle could not forgive him for his indifferences, for his lassitude, for his unwillingness to give it his all.

That is the dark conflict—that exquisite yet tragic tension between the possible and the impossible—that lives within pragmatic idealists.

They are hopelessly stuck in a less than perfect world, in a world in which most people quit long before pragmatic idealists even get started. Yet it is not other people who drive pragmatic idealists to desperation, who are continued disappointments. It is they who disappoint themselves most of all. They are forever lost in their own failings.

As good as they are, they are never good enough—

never smart enough, never disciplined enough, never sensitive enough. Yet, in their minds, they are always on the edge of something—a breakthrough, a discovery, a find of existential importance.

Pragmatic idealists in business know what the drive for excellence is all about. They invent it. They are its slaves. They cannot imagine any other way to live. Excellence is not a word to them. It is not a strategy, but a feeling, a passion—a profound idea. It courses through their veins.

I'm talking about tough stuff.

I'm suggesting that great companies become great companies because they are headed by great people who don't feel their greatness, *and never will.*

Great companies, E-Myth Enterprises, are headed by great people who are possessed by a burning hunger to create something perfect in the world that they can't find in themselves.

And they can't help themselves.

It's not something they do out of choice.

They are completely possessed.

They are caught up by an idea that continually eludes them, that hovers tantalizingly just out of reach, that can't be perfectly seen or apprehended, but that promises to reveal itself at any moment if the seeker will just extend himself or herself one step more.

In other words, the E-Myth Perspective, the desire to create a great company, or a great saxophonist, or a great automobile, or a great garden, is not for the fainthearted, the weak, or the sentimental.

It takes everything one has, and more.
It is both a blessing and a curse.
Understand, I'm not talking about heroes here.
Most often, these people are unbearable to be
    around.
If they are impeccable in one thing, they are often
    disasters in another.
They are walking contradictions.

Rink Babka, for over two decades one of the top ten discus throwers in the world, told me that his coach, Dink Templeton, one of the most brilliant coaches the world has ever known, "smoked like a chimney, drank like a fish, and swore like a trooper." Yet when it came to the sport, there was no one more dedicated, more possessed, more committed to perfection for his boys.

It is no secret that Walt Disney was a dope when it came to business finance. If it had been left up to him, his business would have failed a dozen times.

It is no secret that Ray Kroc held permanent grudges, insulted his people, and was known to throw fits of temper like the worst adolescent.

It is no secret that Steve Jobs controls every aspect of the so-called Apple Experience, from the clean, crisp, no-nonsense design and layout of Apple stores, to the urgent "open me" (yet environmentally sound) sense and simplicity of the packaging of products, to the elegant and utilitarian design of the products themselves.

Yet, while all these things are true, there is brilliance about such people—a vital edge that distinguishes them from everyone else. You can—or could—see it in their eyes.

That vital edge comes from the fact that they are driven by ideas.

Ideas reside at the heart of the E-Myth Perspective.

Those who are possessed by the E-Myth Perspective are driven by ideas.

Ideas are the food by which such people are nourished, revitalized, and given the life they crave—ideas of such awesome size, temper, and quality, that they are compelled to re-create them, to give them physical form, to give them presence, to give them substance, to give them reality in this world.

Discussing his novel *A Good Day to Die*, author Jim Harrison explains that the title was borrowed from Indian lore:

That comes from the Nez Perce saying, the whole idea you have to be morally and spiritually, as a warrior—whether you're a writer or businessperson—you have to live so correctly that you can wake up in the morning and look out and say, "Today is a good day to die." One very rarely is in that kind of shape, but it's a tremendous thing to be able to say.

How many of us have lived "morally and spiritually as a warrior"?

How many of us have lived so correctly, that we could, if faced with death, let go of our lives without regret, completely empty, devoid of shame, regret, longing?

What does it mean to live correctly?
What would a warrior businessperson, a warrior
    merchant, be?
It's not the business at all.
The whole idea falls apart if it's tied down by a
    business.

The whole idea becomes unthinkable if it's tied down by the idea of Cheez Balls, or Ritz Crackers, or Jell-O.

The whole idea of the E-Myth Perspective isn't tied down to the commercial reality of what our business is doing; it exceeds it.

It raises it up.
An E-Myth Enterprise doesn't make Cheez Balls.
Because Cheez Balls are not something a person
    can feel good about.
No matter how hard he or she tries.
And if he or she could feel good about Cheez Balls,
    it's already too late.

No, if there could be such a person as a warrior merchant (and we're just pursuing possibilities here), I would imagine that he or she would be able to discriminate between Cheez Balls and other more worthwhile things.

An essential component of the E-Myth Perspective is that what a business creates—the commodities or products it sells or chooses to develop for sale—is critical to the values inherent in the business itself.

Because making Cheez Balls has no inherent value, and is of value only because of the money it creates, and because creating money by making Cheez Balls must ultimately degrade one's dignity—one's sense of personal human value—the warrior merchant we are speaking about (if there could be such a person) could not live in such a state. He or she would not wish to be found by death in such a state. It most certainly would not be "a good day to die" if that were the case.

How could anybody choose Cheez Balls as their intentional fate?

I've watched an iron man win the Iron Man contest.

I've watched a slight, wiry woman climb straight up a mountain.

I've watched a monster of a man win the heavyweight title by soundly whipping a man-sized monster.

I've watched a whip-fast master defeat another whip-fast master with one stroke in karate.

I've watched a master violinist hold an audience
in thrall.

On the other hand, I've watched Marino Santos
use more of himself, while touching more people more
permanently than any one of these five ever did or ever
could.

Yet, to the world, any one of the five might be considered nobler than Marino Santos, because their efforts
would be considered to be more worthwhile.

I disagree.

I believe that Marino Santos invented a new paradigm
of service for the world.

I believe he heroically exceeded the limits imposed
by the existing paradigm and, in the process, by being
diligent, conscientious, interested, deliberate, and intelligent, holds the potential to positively affect—if all else
goes right—the emotions, standards, behavior, and quality of life of millions of people by his example of doing
ordinary work in such an extraordinary way.

I believe he took more of himself to task than most
people ever will. He extended what he found to the outside world, creating a new model of behavior, a new rigor
of attention, a new level of consciousness, both intense
and relaxed at the same time.

I know in my heart that Marino Santos would never
make Cheez Balls.

You know it, too.

There must have been a moment in time at the beginning of the free market system, when the human mind and the human heart were asked, "Cheez Balls or not, what do you think?"

And the human being responded, "Screw it, Cheez Balls it is."

This was a moment when something inoffensively trivial inserted itself into the human equation as significantly more important than it was; when something much less trivial—something so big in us we couldn't get our arms around it—found no justification for hanging around, so we sat down on the sidelines stuffing Cheez Balls into our faces instead. They were so easy, so available, so tasty—so dead.

What is it about us that makes it so easy to be so
self-indulgent?

What is it about a free market system that seems
to breed Cheez Balls like flies?

What is it about us in a free market system that
never grows tired of yet another variation on
the Cheez Balls theme, whether we're poets,
philosophers, mathematical giants, computer
programmers, dentists, doctors, college professors, truck drivers, or poodle clippers?

In a free market system, somehow "Pass the Cheez Balls, please!" always wins the day.

But, wait a second, Cheez Balls aren't the problem!

It's this thing about dying.

It's this thing about always being prepared to die today.

It's about having lived so impeccably, having lived so correctly, having carried oneself with such presence, such dignity, having lived with such awareness, such inner vitality, such grace, such intensity as if "a fire were raging in your hair."

It's our choice of being that's the problem.

It's that which separates the E-Myth Entrepreneur—and Enterprise—from all the others.

It's the warrior merchant's penchant for living in a state of grace.

I know a man who can sell anything, and has. I'll call him Murray, but that's not his name. (He knows who he is if he is reading this.)

There is something about Murray that disturbs me.

He has the eye of a pirate. You know what I mean: it has a certain slant to it. It shines like a hard black stone caught just right in the sun—as if you could walk the plank for all he cares; it has nothing to do with him.

Yet Murray believes he is exactly the opposite of that.

Murray believes in himself and what he does.

Murray is all business, and business is all Murray.

As I said, he can sell anything, and has.

To Murray, there is no difference between things.

He is totally devoid of values.

But he doesn't believe that about himself.

He believes he has values; he talks about them all
    the time.

He believes that he is a scientist and that he truly
    understands what people want.

He believes that he is a scientist of the passions.

He has made a study of them. He has discovered the words to use to provide people with what he believes they want. He has discovered the way to provide people with the illusion that they're getting what they want. He has found a way to believe that what he does is important. Murray is a magician.

He sells this service to people. He calls it marketing.

Murray doesn't care what they do with it, so long as it interests him. That is one thing that's interesting about Murray: although he will sell anything, he won't sell anything that doesn't interest him. It has to present a unique problem, it has to be difficult to do, it has to present Murray with a real challenge, and it has to have the potential of making Murray an awful lot of money.

If it won't make an awful lot of money for Murray, it doesn't matter how big a challenge it presents.

To Murray, everyone has to be someplace. It really doesn't matter where, as long as it's worth Murray's time.

Murray sits in a big fat chair at the heart of American business.

These words won't let me go.

Attention, concentration.
Intention, discrimination.
Balance, organization.
Excellence, innovation.
Touching the world, communication.

These words are values; these values are words.

They are at the heart of the subject at hand.

Although you might think I'm taking a circuitous route in dealing with the issues of what makes a great business, I'm simply not doing it in a businesslike way.

But that's just the point. *I have never seen a great business that does things in a businesslike way!*

* * *

DESIGNING THE ENTERPRISE:
THE TAKEAWAY POINTS

(Listen to the Podcast version
at MichaeleGerber.com)

■

This is the E-Myth Perspective. Service, excellence, and caring are not something you can do anything about. They are a state of mind. When a business is bereft of such qualities, it is because its founders, its owners, and its managers are bereft of such qualities. They don't care to serve. It doesn't bother them that their performance is less, by far, than excellent. They don't care about the business because they simply don't care at all.

Great companies, E-Myth Enterprises, are headed by great people who are possessed by a burning hunger to create something perfect in the world that they can't find in themselves.

Ideas reside at the heart of the E-Myth Perspective.

Those who are possessed by the E-Myth Perspective are driven by ideas.

* * *

CHAPTER NINE

SHOOTING FOR THE MOON

■

He not busy being born is busy dying.

—Bob Dylan, "It's Alright, Ma (I'm Only Bleeding)"

If bullshit was water, we'd have all drowned by now.

—Anonymous

I want to talk about the word *power* again—a word easily used and just as easily misunderstood.

What is power, after all, but the ability to "do"?

If we are truly to possess the ability to "do" anything—to truly possess power—it goes without saying that we must be conscious, present, awake, and free of all internal and external influences at the moment of "doing."

In short, to "do"—to possess power—requires that we *choose* to "do," that we make a conscious choice.

If one accepts that definition, then those things we do automatically—in reaction to events, feelings, or internal programming—cannot be considered true "doing," in that they are not truly done by *us,* but by our habits.

For our purpose here, that sort of "doing" can more accurately be called "nondoing," or acting out the unconscious. In such cases, "it" did it, you didn't; there was no conscious choice.

It can be argued that most, if not all, of what we "do" is of this sort of "doing," out of our control—just happens reflexively.

Think about it. How many times have you lashed out at someone automatically because he or she triggered an old rage?

You didn't do that, "it" did.

How many times have you repeated a physical act like taking off your shoes, first the left shoe, then the right?

You didn't do that, "it" did.

It's often been said, "I could do that in my sleep."

In fact, we do. More often than we'd care to think.

Okay, here's the problem in a nutshell.

It is my belief that a true E-Myth Enterprise requires an E-Myth Perspective.

And to have an E-Myth Perspective requires an E-Myth Mind.

And my definition of an E-Myth Mind is one that is capable of objectivity.

It is a mind that watches from the outside what is going on in the inside, a mind that can grasp the entirety of the condition in which we find ourselves—*at once.*

It is a mind that can seize the whole.

Imagine all life as we know it operating within a circle.

The objective mind—the E-Myth Mind—would be one that could live outside of that circle, while still living inside of it.

The objective mind would be totally *unidentified* with what's going on inside the circle.

Unfortunately, to possess such a mind would require a level of awakeness, of awareness, of unbuffered honesty, of clarity, that simply does not exist in us today, if it ever did.

And I believe strongly that rather than getting better, our condition is getting worse; that the likelihood of us becoming more objective— that is, less identified—is slim, and growing slimmer all the time.

Although I obviously am not an optimist, neither am I a pessimist. Nor would I call myself a realist; I'm too far gone for that.

But, somewhere in the middle of all this, I find myself with a particularly vexing problem for which I have yet to find a name—a problem that plagues me in everything I do, and everywhere I go, and with everyone I meet. And, lest you doubt me, I do mean *everyone,* no exception.

My problem has to do with the absence of true power.

Everywhere I go, and in everything I do, I am continually confronted by the overwhelmingly obvious and, to me, deeply disturbing fact that all of the people I come into contact with—every last soul—are totally and unconscionably asleep. Gonzo. Out to lunch. On automatic. Unconscious.

In short, unobjective.

Rather than being unidentified with everything going on—that is, objective—everyone I meet is hopelessly identified with what's going on—that is, subjective: hopelessly inseparable from the events of which their lives are made.

In short, I have come to the unhappy conclusion that if the sample I have taken of the world at large is a reasonable approximation of the truth (and I believe an airtight case could be made to support it), then, despite what most of us would like to believe, there is no such thing as someone who could honestly call himself or herself an individual—someone who is capable of living both inside and outside the circle at the very same time, who is capable of achieving a state of true separation, that is, objectivity. If that is so, and I believe with all my heart that it is, then the companies (let alone the lives) of such people are doomed before they even begin.

I believe that is the reason so few companies achieve even a modest degree of success, or, put more directly, why so many companies fail.

It has nothing to do with the absence of business acumen or bad luck, as is commonly supposed. It has more to do with the *unconsciousness* of the people who create them, and the people who manage them, and the people who work in them, and the people who buy from them, and the people who sell to them, and the people who lend to them.

It has to do with *us*.
With *all* of us.
And *only* with us.
With the unconscious condition called human.

If I were traveling in a tight social circle, with limited interaction, among a small, select group, you could justifiably say to me, "Expand your horizons, Michael, and your problems will be solved. Not *all* people are like the ones you've described."

Unfortunately, at least for me (after all, it's *my* problem), that's not the case. I don't travel in a tight social circle. I come into contact with thousands of people each year. A diverse range of people. People who work in every imaginable sector of our society. People who do just about everything people can do in this world of ours. Scientists, craftspeople, artists, mechanics, musicians, businesspeople, ditchdiggers, speakers, politicians, carpenters, bank presidents, writers, technicians, computer programmers, loan officers, managers, millionaires, paupers, great thinkers, and dullards. And, despite all their differences, I find it to be tragically true that all of them—every single last living one of them, without exception—are caught hopelessly and helplessly in the muck and mire of deep, lasting, impenetrable sleep.

They are all hopelessly identified with what they do and with who they think they are.

They are full of themselves.

They find it impossible to separate themselves, for even a moment, from the fools they have learned to play, from the costumes they have grown accustomed to wear.

And this is as true of the positive thinkers I have met as it is of the negative thinkers I have met. It is as true at the far left of the New Age, as it is at the far right of the Old Age.

Whether they be humanists or religionists, whether they be apolitical or deeply political, whether they be conservationists or the opposite, whatever that would be, all of them, every last single one of the people I have met—*yes, I'm talking about you and me*—all of us, are dead-to-the-world asleep.

Nobody I have ever met lives outside the circle.

Every single one of us has an agenda with which we have become inseparably identified; a role that fits us to a tee; a way of moving through the world that has become our persona, our comfort zone, the reflection we see in our moment-to-moment mirror; the personage we continue to convey out there to the rest of the world, and in here to ourselves, saying, over and over again, automatically, without serious question, in a thousand different instants, to everyone and everything, "That's me!"

Until finally, we are our agendas. And in the process, we cease to truly be.

There can be no freedom as long as we live this way.
There can be no true power when one is asleep.
There can be no true responsibility when one operates like a machine.

And so I am not surprised at the dumb conclusions we "business writers" reach.

I am not surprised that, as you search for solutions to your business problems, you are constantly being cajoled to stay *inside* the circle rather than to step *outside* it; that you are constantly being invited to become more identified rather than less identified; that you are continually being offered a new technique—a new rhetoric, a new belief, the newest wisdom, the latest insight—whether it be "megatrends 2015," or Six Sigma, or "New Age thinking," or "the information age," or "the information worker," "excellence," or "creating chaos," or "one-minute managing," or "leadership training," or "win–win relationships," or whatever it's called. Because whoever wrote it is speaking about stuff *inside* the circle, *from* inside the circle, and all one can get from there is more of the same.

It cannot set us free!

For the proof, look around you.

No matter how many new thoughts, no matter how many new ideas, no matter how many new breakthroughs in "human technology" come our way, they all will move us in only one direction, down the street of our sleep into a dream world of delusion, none of them having made a difference, none of them *capable* of making a difference, and none of them *ever will* make a difference for you or for me—not until something in us, in you and me, changes.

The problem is *that we think we're awake.*

That we think we already are objective.

That we think we already are individuals.

That we think we already are free.

That we think that we think!

The problem is that we think we're making decisions all of the time, when in fact we're not.

We have never even learned how to make decisions.

We're dreaming, hopelessly adrift in a sea of reaction to conditions that control, cajole us, romance us, and delude us.

We call these reactions "passion."

We call these reactions "moral indignation."

We call these reactions "desire."

We call these reactions "thoughts," "hope," "interest," and "creativity."

And we end up praising these *reactions,* as though they were *qualities* instead.

We call our reactions everything but what they really are: associations, dreams, neural connections, fantasies.

And then we take one step further—and this is the malevolent step, the deadly step, the step of psychopathology.

We say to ourselves, that since all of our conditioning is habitual, then, to develop ourselves, to become more effective, to become better people, to become more human, all we have to do is develop better habits.

Voilà!

Rather than attempting to come awake, our solution is to become better at *sleeping.*

This is a very complicated problem.

It could go in any direction.

On the one hand, I'm presuming to provide you with a prescription, a template, for business success. On the other hand, I'm telling you why success is *impossible*, given the way you and I are.

What a conundrum!

How do we get around this?

How do we pursue the impossible?

Is this a cul-de-sac, or is there a way through?

The first step in this complicated process is for us to agree about our condition. We must agree that no matter what anyone tells us, no matter how many psychologists we listen to, no matter how many promises experts in enlightenment and human behavior make, no matter how many idealistic, enraptured, New Age songs of hope come our way about the evolution of man—about the civilizing process, about the glorious future that we all thought awaited us in the glorious "Third Millennium" in which we are already several years entrenched, the age of the "empowered individual"—we are not, and have not been becoming, more human as time wears on. We are becoming *less* so—by the minute.

Examples abound.

I walk in a country where violent killings, rapes, robberies, assaults, and burglaries occur every single day. In incomprehensible numbers.

I walk in a country in which the vast majority of high school graduates cannot tell you when Abraham Lincoln served as president, do not know where electricity comes from, cannot calculate the circumference of a circle, cannot read at better than tenth-grade level, cannot even tell you in what state New York City is located.

I walk in a country in which the incidence of battered wives and battered children grows exponentially each year, and in which human abuse so unfathomable, so inhuman, so degrading is more pervasive worldwide than at any other time in history.

I walk in a country in which I have heard that at least 26.2 million of us have a diagnosed mental disorder, in which roughly 50 percent of our marriages end in divorce, and in which at least 1.5 million—one out of every 200—Americans are addicted to cocaine.

I walk in a country—in a world—in which our forests are systematically being destroyed, our water is systematically being contaminated, our air is systematically being poisoned, our wildlife is systematically being annihilated, our pets are systematically being abandoned, our people are systematically being ignored, and our families are systematically being decimated, at ever-increasing rates, with no sign of abatement in any quarter.

I live in a country in which at least 42,000 people are killed every year in automobile accidents.

In which I have heard that 75 percent of our families are dysfunctional.

In which our entertainment has become increasingly more juvenile, increasingly more violent, increasingly more inane.

Walk down the streets of any large city.

Try the subway in New York. Yes, it's better than in the past, but it's still not good.

And this is what the rest of the world is shooting for?

To become more like us?

To trade their sleep for our sleep?

So much for the New Age.

So much for being more human.

We are a walking disgrace.

But, take solace. At least it's not our fault.

We're all sound asleep, for God's sake!

Have you ever watched our Congress in the midst of debate on important issues?

Did you observe how sleep works?

Did you see our lofty representatives' mouths moving, their eyes inert, their limbs flailing away, their empty sleeves, their shoes filled with straw, their empty mouths uttering empty phrases?

Do you understand what was going on?

Did you by chance get a picture of yourself watching, your mouth moving, your eyes inert, your limbs flailing away, your empty sleeves, your shoes filled with straw, your empty mouth uttering empty phrases?

Were you shocked by what you saw?

All of the solutions out there—every last single one

of them, no matter how worthwhile they may sound—
mean *absolutely nothing* if we, the people of this world,
remain the same.

If we continue to think we're awake . . . but we're
not.

If we continue to act as though we are making conscious decisions that we have chosen to be who we are.

But if we see how powerless we have all become—
how much of ourselves we have willingly given up; how
ready we have been to live in this unconscious state,
automatically walking through our lives as though fast
asleep, doing our routines, our tap dances, singing our
little songs, and repeating our little rituals that long ago
lost any semblance of meaning or grace—if we can see
that; if for one shuddering, remarkable instant we can
recognize that we are asleep, and we can see that we are
passively reciting our own dogmas, our own prescriptions, our own automata, our own ritualized beliefs,
then our purpose comes fleetingly to life.

It is at the miraculous instant when we first see
ourselves—when we recognize how programmed we
are and how badly we need to be reprogrammed. It
is at this power-packed instant when we come face-
to-face with ourselves, not from inside the circle, but
from outside the circle—looking down, so to speak. It
is at this instant when anything is possible, and only at
this instant, when for a fleeting moment we are wide
awake.

This is the instant of awakening.
It is an instant of intense energy, of intense life, of
    intense vitality.
It is the instant within which the possibility of
    true freedom can be truly felt and born.

And so my prescription begins and ends with *us*.
My prescription says that, to build an E-Myth Enterprise, one must be interested in far more than just
business.

■

**Mere business cannot hold the interest of
an intelligent person for long.
One must be interested in the
dignity of one's own life.
And of the lives of those around us.**

One must be interested in doing what one does with
the utmost attention, with the utmost care, with the
utmost interest, and with the utmost engagement.
One must set standards: difficult standards, standards that rise above the ordinary, standards that one
would be willing to share with the world as exem-
plars of human behavior, standards that one would
be willing to publish for all people to see, standards
that one would be willing to be held accountable for

and would be eager to be measured against always and forever.

* * *

One must be interested in how things look, and how things feel, and how things work, and then, finally, in the money. One must know that the money, while not key, is a serious consideration, but only a consideration. It is not the primary reason or a justification for being in business.

One must forget the economic model of reality.

For an E-Myth Enterprise, there is no economic model. The economic model is a myth.

For an E-Myth Enterprise, there are only people, and cosmic forces that none of us understands, and Whatever, or Whoever, created all this.

One must pay attention to people: to what is imprisoning them; to what is frustrating them; to what is inhibiting them; to what is restraining them; to what is depriving them of a rich, energizing, intelligent, and forceful life.

In order to pay attention to others, one must be conscious of oneself. One must be honest with oneself. One must continually watch oneself.

No excuses.
No defenses.

No lies.
No dishonesty.
No exit.

One must become a soldier on the conscious front.

I'm not saying that to build an E-Myth Enterprise one must *be* conscious—that's too much for anyone to ask.

What I am saying, however, is that one must *wish* to be conscious.

One must wish to be whole.

One must wish to be objective.

One must wish to be impartial.

One must wish to be detached.

One must wish to be free of the automatic responses, the unconscious behavior that fills each of our days.

One must wish to be human in the fullest sense of that word.

When I think of John Anderson . . .

When I think of Mary Conner Brown . . .

When I think of Marino Santos . . .

When I think of Merle . . .

When I think of each extraordinary small business owner I have had the privilege to work with since I started my business thirteen years ago . . .

When I think of all that, I think of the wish that saw us all through.

Not the wish to be successful—that was never it for any of us and never will be—but the wish to do what we set out to do in the most human way possible.

The wish to be true to something higher than the multitude of competing priorities that continually drag us down to earth.

The wish to touch something quieter, finer, deeper, more resolute, more compassionate, more courageous, more challenging, more worthy, more human—more dignified—in the course of our lives.

It is my contention that no business, no matter what it does, can become great if its people wish for anything less than these things.

An E-Myth Enterprise is a business that takes personal responsibility for the condition of the world it finds itself in; for the condition of the people with whom it interacts; for the condition of their children and their children's children; for the condition of the very quality of life itself.

A business with conscience.

That is, I believe, the only mission worthy of the name.

To create a world in which people are present, honest, open, and alive.

To create a world in which people make conscious decisions in good conscience.

That is what shooting for the moon is all about.

And one cannot do it in one's sleep.

It requires all we have.

And it requires it *now*.

*   *   *

DESIGNING THE ENTERPRISE:
THE TAKEAWAY POINTS

**(Listen to the Podcast version
at MichaelEGerber.com)**

■

An E-Myth Enterprise is a business that takes personal responsibility for the condition of the world it finds itself in; for the condition of the people with whom it interacts; for the condition of their children and their children's children; for the condition of the very quality of life itself.

A business with conscience.
That is, I believe, the only mission worthy of the
   name.
To accomplish this mission requires all that we
   have.

To Build *Your* E-Myth Enterprise . . .
Go To MichaelEGerber.com

■

Because Michael Gerber *is* The E-Myth Coach . . .

■

For immediate help and a *Free*
E-Myth Enterprise CD, call the Michael Gerber
Team at 760-752-7912

INDEX

THE COMPLETE ENTREPRENEUR'S LIBRARY

THE E-MYTH
REVISITED
*Why Most Small
Businesses Don't
Work and What to
Do About It*

ISBN 978-0-88-730728-7 (paperback)

Also available as a CD, ebook, and downloadable audio.

Learn the vital, often overlooked distinction between working *on* your business and working *in* your business.

E-MYTH MASTERY
*The Seven Essential
Disciplines for
Building a World
Class Company*

ISBN 978-0-06-072323-1 (paperback)

Also available as a hardcover, CD, ebook, and downloadable audio.

Presenting practical exercises to help small business owners recover their vision and passion, Gerber clears a path for getting back to the basic disciplines for business success.

AWAKENING THE ENTREPRENEUR WITHIN
*How Ordinary People Can Create
Extraordinary Companies*

ISBN 978-0-06-156814-5 (hardcover)

Also available as a CD, ebook, and downloadable audio.

Join Gerber in the Dreaming Room, where he will help you shape your dream into a viable, economically successful company.

THE E-MYTH CONTRACTOR
*Why Most Contractors' Businesses Don't
Work and What to Do About It*

ISBN 978-0-06-093846-8 (paperback)

Also available as an ebook.

Gerber applies his E-Myth Revolution specifically to contractors—the largest group of clients he serves.

THE E-MYTH MANAGER
*Why Most Managers Aren't Effective and
What to Do About It*

ISBN 978-0-88-730959-5 (paperback)

Also available as an ebook.

Gerber offers a fresh, provacative alternative to management as we know it.

THE E-MYTH PHYSICIAN
*Why Most Medical Practices Don't
Work and What to Do About It*

ISBN 978-0-06-093840-6 (paperback)

Also available as an ebook.

Gerber shares powerful insights that will lead independent physicians to successful practices and enriched lives.

Available wherever books are sold, and at www.michaelegerber.com.

Harper
Business